Contents

MW00578725

2
5
8
10
12
14
16
18
21
24
26
28
33
36
38
40
42
44
46
48
50
51
52
53
54

Embellished Elf Hat & Wristers

Sizes
Sized for Small, Medium, Large.
Shown in size Medium.

Measurements
Hat
- **Circumference** 18 (20, 22)"/45.5 (51, 56)cm

Wrister
- **Circumference** 6½ (7½, 8)"/16.5 (19, 20.5)cm

Gauge
14 sts and 22 rnds to 4"/10cm over St st using size 9 (5.5mm) dpns.
Take time to check your gauge.

Stitch Glossary
M1 (make 1) Insert left needle from front to back into the horizontal strand between the last st worked and the next st on left needle. Knit this strand through the back loop to twist the st.
M1R (make 1 right) Insert left needle from back to front into the horizontal strand between the last st worked and the next st on left needle. Knit this strand through the front loop to twist the st.

YARN 5
- 5¼oz/150g, 245yd/225m of any bulky weight wool blend in purple (MC)
- 1¾oz/50g, 80yd/75m in light purple (A) and light olive (B)
- Small amount of worsted weight yarn in teal green (C) and dark pink (D) (for embroidery)

NEEDLES
- One set (4) size 9 (5.5mm) double-pointed needles (dpns) or size to obtain gauge

NOTIONS
- Stitch marker
- Tapestry needle

Hat
Crown
With dpn and MC, cast on 9 sts, leaving a long tail for sewing. Divide sts over 3 needles. Join, taking care not to twist sts on needles and pm for beg of rnds.
Rnd 1 Knit.
Rnd 2 [K1, M1, k2] 3 times—12 sts.
Rnd 3 [Sl 1, k3] 3 times.
Rnd 4 [K1, M1, k3] 3 times—15 sts.
Rnd 5 [Sl 1, k4] 3 times.
Rnd 6 [K1, M1, k4] 3 times—18 sts.
Rnd 7 [Sl 1, k5] 3 times.
Rnd 8 [K1, M1, k5] 3 times—21 sts.
Rnd 9 [Sl 1, k6] 3 times.
Rnd 10 [K1, M1, k6] 3 times—24 sts.
Rnd 11 [Sl 1, k7] 3 times.
Rnd 12 [K1, M1, k7] 3 times—27 sts.
Rnd 13 [Sl 1, k8] 3 times.
Rnd 14 [K1, M1, k8] 3 times—30 sts.
Rnd 15 [Sl 1, k9] 3 times. Cont to work in this manner, inc 3 sts every other rnd and working 1 more st between sl sts every other rnd until there are 63 (72, 78) sts on dpns. Cont to work as foll:
Next rnd *Sl 1, k20 (23, 25); rep from * around.
Next rnd Knit.
Rep last 2 rnds until piece measures 10 (10½, 11)"/25.5 (26.5, 28)cm from beg.

I-Cord Edging
With RS facing and A, cast 3 sts onto LH needle. Work I-cord edging as foll: *with A, k2, then k2tog tbl (last A st and first MC st on LH needle); place the 3 sts on RH needle just knitted onto LH needle; rep from * until 3 sts rem. Bind off rem 3 sts.

Finishing
Thread beg tail in tapestry needle. Weave tail around opening at top of crown. Pull tog tightly and secure end. Sew ends of I-cord edging tog.

Embroidery
Referring to diagram, use B to embroider three 6-petal lazy daisy stitch flowers on front of hat. Using C, embroider two lazy daisy stitch leaves for each flower. Using D, embroider a 5-wrap bullion knot in center of each flower.

Tassel
Cut four 9"/23cm strands each of MC, A and B. Use tapestry needle to thread strands through top of hat. Tie strands in a square knot.

Wristers (make 2)
With dpns and A, cast on 24 (28, 28) sts, dividing sts over 3 needles. Join, taking care not to twist sts on needles and pm for beg of rnds. Work in k2, p2 rib for 3 (3½, 3½)"/7.5 (9, 9)cm, dec 2 (2, 0) sts evenly spaced—22 (26, 28) sts. Change to MC. Cont in St st and work even for 4 (5, 5) rnds.

Thumb Gusset
Rnd 1 K11 (13, 14), pm, M1, M1R, pm, k11 (13, 14)—24 (28, 30) sts.
Rnd 2 Knit.
Rnd 3 K to first marker, sl marker, M1R, k to

Paul Amato for Lvarepresents.com

Embellished Elf Hat & Wristers

next marker, M1, sl marker, k to end—26 (30, 32) sts.

Rnd 4 Knit.

Rep last two rnds 3 (3, 4) times more—32 (36, 40) sts.

Next rnd K11 (13, 14), bind off next 10 (10, 12) sts, k to end.

Hand

Knit 4 rnds over 22 (26, 28) sts. Cont in k1, p1 rib for 4 (6, 6) rnds. Bind off losely in rib.

FINISHING

Embroidery

Referring to diagram, use B to embroider one 5-petal lazy daisy stitch flower to front of each wrister. Using C, embroider two or three lazy daisy stitch leaves for each flower. Using D, embroider a 5-wrap bullion knot in center of each flower. ■

5-Petal flower

6-Petal flower

Stitch key

Lazy daisy st

5-Wrap bullion knot

Color key

Light olive (B)

Teal green (C)

Dark pink (D)

Do the Twist

Sizes

Hat Sized for Adult Woman.

Capelet Sized for Small/Medium, Large/X-Large, XX-Large.

Shown in size Small/Medium.

Measurements

Hat

- **Circumference** 21"/53cm

Capelet

- **Width at lower edge** 59 (62¾, 66½)"/150 (159, 169)cm
- **Length** 16 (16, 17½)"/40.5 (40.5, 44.5)cm

Gauges

Hat

16 sts and 26 rnds to 4"/10cm over cable pat in section 1 using size 9 (5.5mm) needles.

Capelet

17 sts and 26 rnds to 4"/10cm over St st using size 9 (5.5mm) needles.

Take time to check your gauges.

K2, P2 Rib

(multiple of 4 sts)

Rnd 1 *K2, p2; rep from * around.

Rnd 2 K the knit sts and p the purl sts.

Rep rnd 2 for k2, p2 rib.

Stitch Glossary

10-st LC Sl 5 sts to cn and hold to front, k5, k5 from cn.

8-st LC Sl 4 sts to cn and hold to front, k4, k4 from cn.

6-st LC Sl 3 sts to cn and hold to front, k3, k3 from cn.

4-st LC Sl 2 sts to cn and hold to front, k2, k2 from cn.

Hat

YARN (4)

- 1¾oz/50g, 109yd/98m of any worsted weight wool tweed

KNITTING NEEDLES

- One set (5) each sizes 7 and 9 (4.5 and 5.5mm) double-pointed needles (dpns) *or size to obtain gauge*

ADDITIONAL MATERIALS

- Cable needle (cn)
- Stitch marker

Capelet

YARN (4)

- 10½oz/300g, 654yd/588m (12¼oz/350g, 763yd/686m; 14oz/400g, 872yd/784m) of any worsted weight wool tweed

KNITTING NEEDLES

- Two size 9 (5.5mm) circular needles, one each 16"/40cm and 32"/80cm long *or size to obtain gauge*

ADDITIONAL MATERIALS

- Cable needle (cn)
- Stitch marker
- Tapestry needle

Hat

With smaller dpn, cast on 84 sts. Divide sts evenly over 4 needles (21 sts on each needle). Join, taking care not to twist sts, and place marker for beg of rnd.

Work in k2, p2 rib for 3"/7.5cm.

Change to larger dpn.

Section 1

Rnds 1 and 3 Knit.

Rnds 2 and 4 [K2, p2, k6, p2] 7 times around.

Rnd 5 [K4, 6-st LC, k2] 7 times around.

Rnd 6 Rep rnd 2. Rep rnds 1–6 twice more.

Work rnds 1–5 once more.

Next (dec) rnd [K2, p2, ssk, k2, k2tog, p2] 7 times around—70 sts.

Section 2

Rnd 1 Knit.

Rnds 2 and 4 [K2, p2, k4, p2] 7 times around.

Rnd 3 [K4, 4-st LC, k2] 7 times around.

Rep rnds 1–4 once more.

Next (dec) rnd [K4, ssk, k2tog, k2] 7 times around—56 sts.

Section 3

Rnd 1 *K2, p2; rep from * around.

Do the Twist

Rnd 2 Knit.
Rep rnds 1 and 2 until piece measures 7¾"/19.5cm from beg, end with a rnd 2.
Next (dec) rnd *K2, p2tog; rep from * around—42 sts. Knit 1 rnd.
Next (dec) rnd *K1, ssk; rep from * around—28 sts. Knit 1 rnd.
Next (dec) rnd K2tog around—14 sts.
Cut yarn and thread through rem sts. Pull to close top and secure.

Capelet

With longer circular needle, cast on 256 (272, 288) sts. Join rnd taking care not to twist sts. Place marker for beg of rnd and sl marker every rnd.
Work in k2, p2 rib for 3 rnds.
Rnd 1 Knit.
Rnd 2 *K2, p2, k10, p2; rep from * around.
Rep last 2 rnds until piece measures 3"/7.5cm from beg, end with a rnd 2.

Section 1

Rnd 1 *K4, 10-st LC, k2; rep from * around.
Rnds 2, 4, 6, 8 and 10 *K2, p2, k10, p2; rep from * around.
Rnds 3, 5, 7 and 9 Knit.
Rep rnds 1–10 for 2 (2, 3) times more; work rnds 1–6 once more.
Next (dec) rnd *K4, ssk, k6, k2tog, k2; rep from * around—224 (238, 252) sts.
Next rnd *K2, p2, k8, p2; rep from * around.

Section 2

Rnd 1 *K4, 8-st LC, k2; rep from * around.
Rnds 2, 4, 6 and 8 *K2, p2, k8, p2; rep from * around.
Rnds 3, 5 and 7 Knit.
Rnd 9 Rep rnd 1.
Rnd 10 Rep rnd 2.
Next (dec) rnd *K4, ssk, k4, k2tog, k2; rep from * around—192 (204, 216) sts.
Next rnd * K2, p2, k6, p2; rep from * around.

Section 3

Rnd 1 Knit.
Rnds 2, 4 and 6 *K2, p2, k6, p2; rep from * around.
Rnd 3 *K4, 6-st LC, k2; rep from * around.
Rnd 5 Knit.
Rep rnds 1–6 once more.
Next (dec) rnd *K4, ssk, k2, k2tog, k2; rep from * around—160 (170, 180) sts.
Next rnd *K2, p2, k4, p2; rep from * around.

Section 4

Rnd 1 *K4, 4-st LC, k2; rep from * around.
Rnds 2 and 4 *K2, p2, k4, p2; rep from * around.
Rnd 3 Knit.
Rep rnds 1–4 until piece measures approx 13 (13, 14½)"/33 (33, 37)cm from beg, end with a rnd 1.
Next (dec) rnd *K4, ssk, k2tog, k2; rep from * around 128 (136, 144) sts.
Cont in k2, p2 rib for 3"/7.5cm. Bind off all sts purlwise. ■

Paul Amato for Lvarepresents.com

Flowered Hat & Wristers

Sizes
Sized for Small, Medium, Large.
Shown in size Medium.

Measurements
- **Hat Circumference**
  18 (20, 22)"/45.5 (51, 56)cm
- **Wrister Circumference**
  6½ (7½, 8)"/16.5 (19, 20.5)cm

Gauges
- 20 sts and 28 rnds to 4"/10cm over St st using size 8 (5mm) circular needle.
- 22 sts and 32 rnds to 4"/10cm over St st using size 5 (3.75mm) dpns.

Take time to check your gauges.

Stitch Glossary
M1 (make 1) Insert left needle from front to back into the horizontal strand between the last st worked and the next st on left needle. Knit this strand through the back loop to twist the st.

M1R (make 1 right) Insert left needle from back to front into the horizontal strand between the last st worked and the next st on left needle. Knit this strand through the front loop to twist the st.

Hat
With circular needle and MC, cast on 88 (100, 108) sts. Join, taking care not to twist sts on needle and pm for beg of rnds. Work in k2, p2 rib for 1"/2.5cm, inc 2 (0, 2) sts evenly spaced around last rnd—90 (100, 110) sts. Cont in St st until piece measures 5 (5½, 6)"/12.5 (14, 15)cm from beg.

YARN (4)
- 3½oz/100g, 220yd/201m of any worsted weight variegated wool yarn in purple multi (MC)
- 3½oz/100g, 220yd/201m of any worsted weight wool blend yarn in magenta (CC)

Needles
- One size 8 (5mm) circular needle, 16"/40cm long *or size to obtain gauge*
- One set each (4) sizes 5 and 8 (3.75 and 5mm) double-pointed needles (dpns) *or sizes to obtain gauge*

Notions
- Size G/6 (4mm) crochet hook
- Stitch marker
- Scrap yarn
- Tapestry needle

Shape Crown
Note Change to dpns when sts no longer comfortably fit on circular needle.

Rnd 1 [K7, SK2P] 9 (10, 11) times—72 (80, 88) sts.

Rnds 2–4 Knit.

Rnd 5 [K5, SK2P] 9 (10, 11) times—54 (60, 66) sts.

Rnds 6–8 Knit.

Rnd 9 [K3, SK2P] 9 (10, 11) times—36 (40, 44) sts.

Rnd 10 Knit.

Rnd 11 [K1, SK2P] 9 (10, 11) times—18 (20, 22) sts.

Rnd 12 Knit.

Rnd 13 K 0 (1, 0), *k1, k2tog; rep from * around, end k 0 (1, 1)—12 (14, 15) sts.

Cut yarn leaving 8"/20.5cm tail and thread through rem sts. Pull tog tightly and secure end.

Wristers (make 2)
With size 5 (3.75mm) dpns and MC, cast on 32 (36, 40) sts dividing sts over 3 needles. Join, taking care not to twist sts on needles and pm for beg of rnds. Work in k2, p2 rib for 10 (12, 14) rnds.

Next (inc) rnd Knit, inc 4 (6, 6) sts evenly spaced—36 (42, 46) sts.

Cont in St st and work even for 7 (8, 9) rnds.

Thumb Gusset
Rnd 1 K17 (20, 22), pm, k2, pm, k17 (20, 22).

Rnd 2 K to first marker, sl marker, M1, k to next marker, M1R, sl marker, k to end—38 (44, 48) sts.

Rnd 3 Knit. Rep last 2 rnds 4 (5, 5) times more—46 (54, 58) sts. Knit next 5 rnds.

Hand
Next (joining) rnd K17 (20, 22), place 12 (14, 14) thumb sts on scrap yarn, cast on 2 sts, k17 (20, 22) sts—36 (42, 46) sts. Knit next 5 rnds. Cont in k1, p1 rib for 4 rnds. Bind off in rib.

Thumb Opening
Place 12 (14, 14) thumb gusset sts over 2 needles.

Next rnd Join yarn and knit across sts, then with 3rd needle pick up and k 1 st in first cast-on st of hand, pm, pick up and k 1 st in last cast-on st of hand—14 (16, 16) sts. Divide sts evenly over 3 dpns. Join and pm for beg of rnds. Knit next 2 rnds.

Next (dec) rnd K to 2 sts before first marker, ssk, sl marker, k2tog, k to end—12 (14, 14) sts. Knit next rnd. Cont in k1, p1 rib for 4 rnds. Bind off in rib.

Flowers (make 3)

With CC, ch 5. Join ch with a sl st forming a ring.

Rnd 1 (RS) *Ch 6, sc in ring; rep from * around 4 times more—5 ch-6 lps.

Rnd 2 *Work (sc, 5 dc, sc) in next ch-6 lp; rep from * around 4 times more, join rnd with a sl st in first sc—5 petals.

Rnd 3 *Ch 6, sc in ring between next 2 sc of rnd 1; rep from * around 4 times more, join rnd with a sl st in first sc—5 ch-6 lps.

Rnd 4 Rep rnd 2.

Rnd 5 Skip first sc of rnd 1, *ch 6, sc in ring between next 2 sc of rnd 1, skip next 2 sc of rnd 1; rep from * around 4 times more, join rnd with a sl st in first sc—5 ch-6 lps. Fasten off.

Finishing

Sew one flower each to hat and wristers. Tack down each petal of rnds 2 and 4. ■

Paul Amato for Lvarepresents.com

Lacy Eyelet Hat & Scarf

Sizes

Hat is sized for Child's, Women's X-small/Small, Women's Medium/Large.
Shown in Women's X-small/Small.

Measurements

- **Hat circumference** 16 (17½, 19¼)"/40.5 (44.5, 48.5)cm (unstretched)
- **Scarf** 8" x 58½"/20.5cm x 147cm

Gauge

20 sts and 24 rows to 4"/10cm over eyelet pat foll chart using size 8 (5mm) needles.
Take time to check your gauge.

YARN
- 12oz/34g, 630yd/576m of any worsted weight variegated wool in orange multi

KNITTING NEEDLES
- One pair size 8 (5mm) needles for scarf *or size to obtain gauge*
- Size 8 (5mm) circular needle 16"/40cm long and one set (5) double-pointed needles (dpns) size 8 (5mm) for hat *or size to obtain gauge*

ADDITIONAL MATERIALS
- Stitch marker for hat
- Tapestery needle

Hat

With circular needle, cast on 80 (88, 96) stitches. Join, taking care not to twist sts on needle. Place marker for end of rnd and sl marker every rnd.
Work in k1, p1 rib for 1¾"/4.5cm. Work in St st for 3 rnds.
Work eyelet pat chart until piece measures 5 (5½, 6)"/12.5 (14, 15)cm from beg.
Note Transfer sts to dpn when there are not enough to fit on circular needle.

Shape Top

Rnd 1 K6, k2tog; rep from * around—70 (77, 84) sts.
Rnd 2 Knit.
Rnd 3 *K5, k2tog; rep from * around—60 (66, 72) sts.
Rnd 4 Knit.
Rnd 5 *K4, k2tog; rep from * around—50 (55, 60) sts.
Rnd 6 *K3, k2tog; rep from * around—40 (44, 48) sts.
Rnd 7 Knit.
Rnd 8 *K2, k2tog; rep from * around—30 (33, 36) sts.
Rnd 9 Knit.
Rnd 10 *K1, k2tog; rep from * around—20 (22, 24) sts.
Rnd 11 Knit.
Rnd 12 *K2tog; rep from * around—10 (11, 12) sts.
Cut yarn leaving a 12"/30cm tail, thread through remaining sts, cinch tightly to close.

Scarf

Cast on 45 sts. Work in k1, p1 rib for 2½"/6.5cm ending with a RS row.
Next row (WS) Cont rib over first 9 sts, p into front and back of next st, p26, cont rib over last 9 sts—46 sts.
Next row (RS) Cont rib over 9 sts, k28, cont rib to end.
Next row Cont rib over 9 sts, p28, cont rib to end. Keeping first and last 9 sts in rib, work center 28 sts in eyelet pat chart until piece measures 56"/143.5cm from beg, end with a chart row 8.
Work k1, p1 rib over all sts for 2½"/6.5cm.
Bind off in rib. ■

EYELET PATTERN

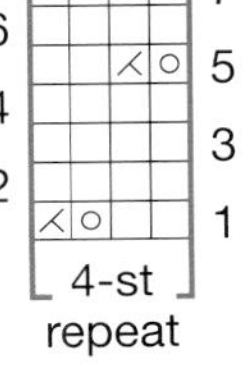

STITCH KEY
- ☐ K on RS, p on WS
- ⧄ K2tog
- ⊡ Yo

Paul Amato for Lvarepresents.com

Good as Gold

Measurements

Hat

- **Circumference** 21½"/54.5cm
- **Length (with folded brim)** 8½"/21.5cm

Cowl

- **Circumference** 31"/78.5cm
- **Length** 12"/30.5cm

Gauges

Hat

18 sts and 27 rnds to 4"/10cm over St st using larger needles.

Cowl

17 sts and 24 rnds to 4"/10cm over rib pat using size 7 (4.5mm) needle.

Take time to check your gauge.

Stitch Glossary

Rib Pattern (over a multiple of 11 sts)

Rnd 1 *K5, p1, k5; rep from * around.

Rep rnd 1 for rib pat.

Hat

YARN (4)

- 3½oz/100g, 244yd/224m of any worsted weight wool tweed in gold

KNITTING NEEDLES

- One set (5) double-pointed needles (dpns) each sizes 5 and 7 (3.75 and 4.5mm) *or size to obtain gauge*

Cowl

YARN (4)

- 7oz/200g, 488yd/448m of any worsted weight wool tweed in gold

KNITTING NEEDLES

- Size 7 (4.5mm) circular needle, 24"/60cm long *or size to obtain gauge*

ADDITIONAL MATERIALS

- Stitch markers

Hat

Brim

With smaller dpn, cast on 96 sts. Divide sts evenly over 4 needles (24 sts on each needle). Join, taking care not to twist sts. Place marker for beg of rnd and slip marker every rnd. Work in k2, p2 rib for 7"/18cm. Change to larger dpns and work in St st knitting every rnd (**Note** You will be working the wrong side of hat facing you) for 3"/7.5cm.

Shape Crown

Dec rnd 1 [K14, k2tog] 6 times—90 sts.

K 1 rnd.

Dec rnd 2 [K13, k2tog] 6 times—84 sts.

K 1 rnd. Rep last 2 rnds, working 1 less st between decs every dec rnd, 3 times more—66 sts.

Cont to dec 6 sts as before every rnd 10 times—6 sts. K 1 rnd. Cut yarn, draw through rem sts and secure.

Finishing

Turn hat inside out so that purl side of crown shows. Fold ribbed brim twice to right side (see photo).

Cowl

Note

Cowl is knit in the round on the wrong side, then folded in half on the right side.

Cast on 132 sts. Join, taking care not to twist sts.

Place marker for beg of rnd and slip marker every rnd.

Work in rib pat for 24"/61cm. Bind off.

Finishing

Fold cowl in half so that the purl side shows. ■

Paul Amato for Lvarepresents.com

Fair Isle & Stripes Set

Measurements

Hat

- **Circumference** 21"/53.5cm
- **Length** 8"/20.5cm

Scarf

Approx 5½ x 65"/14 x 165cm

Gauges

Hat

20 sts and 26 rnds to 4"/10cm over St st using larger needles.

Scarf

30 sts and 26 rows to 4"/10cm over k1, p1 rib using size 7 (4.5mm) needles.

Take time to check your gauges.

Stitch Glossary

K1, P1 Rib

(over an even number of sts)

Row 1 (RS) Sl 1 purlwise, *k1, p1; rep from *, end k1.

Row 2 Sl 1 purlwise, k the knit sts and p the purl sts.

Rep row 2 for k1, p1 rib.

Hat

YARN (4)

- 1¾oz/50g, 91yd/87m of any worsted weight wool blend in cadet blue (A) and shadow gray (B)

KNITTING NEEDLES

- One each sizes 5 and 7 (3.75 and 4.5mm) circular needles, 16"/40cm long *or size to obtain gauge*
- One set (5) size 5 (3.75mm) double-pointed needles (dpns)

ADDITIONAL MATERIALS

- 4 stitch markers
- Tapestry needle

Scarf

YARN (4)

- 7oz/200g, 364yd/348m of any worsted weight wool blend in shadow gray (A)
- 1¾oz/50g, 91yd/87m in cadet blue (B)

KNITTING NEEDLES

- One pair size 7 (4.5mm) needles *or size to obtain gauge*

Hat

Notes

1 When working chart pat, carry color not in use loosely on WS of work.

2 When working chart pat, pick up B strand under A strand.

With smaller circular needle and A, cast on 96 sts. Join, being careful not to twist sts and place marker for beg of rnd. *K1, p1; rep from * around for k1, p1 rib until piece measures 1"/2.5cm from beg.

Next rnd *K11, kfb, rep from * around—104 sts. Change to larger needle and B. Knit 2 rounds.

Begin Chart

Work in St st (knit every rnd) foll chart, working 8-st rep 13 times around until rnd 12 of chart is complete. K 2 rnds B. Cut B. Change to A. Cont in St st until cap measures 5"/12.5cm from beg.

Shape Crown

Note Change to dpns when sts no longer fit comfortably on circular needle.

Next rnd *K26, pm, rep from * twice more, k to end of rnd.

Next (dec) rnd *K2tog, k to 2 sts before next marker, ssk, sl marker, rep from * 3 times more—96 sts.

Next rnd Knit.

Rep dec rnd every other rnd 8 times more—32 sts. Then, rep dec rnd every rnd 3 times more—8 sts. Cut yarn, leaving a long tail. Thread tail through rem sts twice and pull tight.

Finishing

Block Fair Isle band gently if necessary.

Scarf

Notes

1 Slip the first st of each row purlwise for an even edge.

2 Carry colors up the side when working stripe sections.

With A, cast on 42 sts. Work in k1, p1 rib for 14 rows, taking care to slip first st each row. Join B. Cont in rib as established, work [2 rows B, 2 rows A] 6 times. Cut B. Cont in pat with A only until piece measures 59½"/151cm from beg. Join B. Work [2 rows B, 2 rows A] 6 times. Cut B. With A, work 12 rows more. Bind off in rib. ■

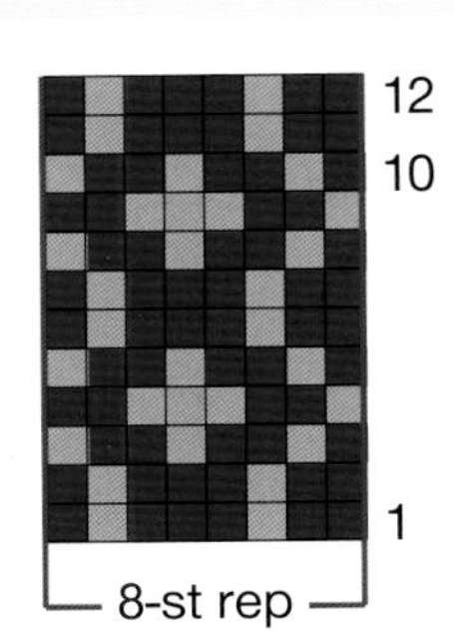

COLOR KEY

- ■ Cadet blue (A)
- ■ Shadow (B)

Paul Amato for Lvarepresents.com

Sideways Cabled Set

Measurements

Hat

- **Circumference** 17"/43cm
- **Length** 8"/20.5cm

Gloves

- **Circumference** 7"/18cm
- **Length** 6½"/16.5cm

Gauge

33 sts and 43 rows to 4"/10cm over cable pat using size 4 (3.5mm) needles.
Take time to check your gauge.

Cable Pattern

(multiple of 9 sts plus 3)
Rows 1, 3 and 7 (RS) Knit.
Row 2 and all WS rows K3, *p6, k3; rep from * to end.
Row 5 K3, *6-st LC (sl 3 sts to cn and hold to front, k3, k3 from cn), k3; rep from * to end.
Row 8 Rep row 2.
Rep rows 1–8 for cable pat.

YARN (2)
- 3½oz/100g, 416yd/380m of any fingering weight wool in orange multi

KNITTING NEEDLES
- One pair size 4 (3.5mm) needles *or size to obtain gauge*
- One set (4) size 4 (3.5mm) double-pointed needles (dpns)

ADDITIONAL MATERIALS
- Cable needle (cn)
- Stitch markers
- Scrap yarn
- Tapestry needle

Hat

Note Hat is worked sideways and seamed. The crown is then picked up and worked from one side edge, the brim from the opposite edge.
Cast on 48 sts. Work rows 1–8 of cable pat until piece measures approx 17"/43cm from beg, end with a row 8. Bind off.
Sew cast-on edge to bound-off edge.

Crown

With RS facing and dpn, pick up and k 90 sts along one side edge (this becomes upper edge). Divide sts evenly on dpn, join and place marker (pm) for beg of rnd.
Rnd 1 [K2tog, k7] 10 times—80 sts.
Rnd 2 Knit.
Rnd 3 [K2tog, k6] 10 times—70 sts.
Rnd 4 Knit.
Cont in this way, working 1 less st after each dec every other rnd 5 times more—10 sts.
Cut yarn and thread through rem sts twice.
Fasten off.

Brim

With RS facing and dpn, pick up and k 92 sts evenly along lower edge. Divide sts evenly on needles, join and pm for beg of rnd.
Rnd 1 *K2, p2; rep from * around. Rep this rnd 5 times more. Bind off loosely in pat.

Gloves

Note Gloves are worked sideways and seamed. Upper edge and cuff are then picked up and worked.
Cast on 30 sts. Work rows 1–8 of cable pat for approx 7"/18cm from beg, end with a row 8.
Next row (RS) Bind off 11 sts, work 8 sts in pat and place on scrap yarn for thumb, bind off rem 11 sts. Sew first and last 11 sts of bound-off row to first and last 11 sts of cast-on row, leaving center 8 sts open for thumb.

Thumb

Place sts from scrap yarn on dpn, pick up and k 2 sts in seam, 8 sts along cast-on edge, 2 sts in seam—20 sts. Divide evenly on dpn, join and place marker (pm) for beg of rnd.
Rnd 1 *K2, p2; rep from * around. Rep this rnd 4 times more for k2, p2 rib.
Bind off loosely in pat.

Upper edge

With RS facing and dpn, pick up and k 48 sts evenly along top edge (either side edge of cabled piece can be top). Divide sts evenly on dpn, join and pm for beg of rnd. Work in k2, p2 rib for 7 rnds. Bind off loosely in pat.

Cuff

With RS facing and dpn, pick up and k 40 sts evenly along lower edge. Divide sts evenly on dpn, join and pm for beg of rnd. Work in k2, p2 rib for 18 rnds. Bind off loosely in pat. ■

Paul Amato for Lvarepresents.com

Cables & Ribbing Set

MEASUREMENTS

Hat

- **Circumference (slightly stretched)** 16"/51cm
- **Length (with brim folded)** 8"/20.5cm

Mittens

- **Hand circumference** 8"/20.5cm
- **Length** 10"/25.5cm

Gauge

26 sts and 28 rows to 4"/10cm over k2, p2 rib using size 7 (4.5mm) needles.
Take time to check your gauge.

Stitch Glossary

2-st RC Sl 1 st to cn, hold to back; on RS, k1, k1 from cn; on WS, p1, p1 from cn.
2-st LC Sl 1 st to cn, hold to front; on RS, k1, k1 from cn; on WS, p1, p1 from cn.
4-st RC Sl 2 sts to cn, hold to back, k2, k2 from cn.
4-st LC Sl 2 sts to cn, hold to front, k2, k2 from cn.
4-st RPC Sl 2 sts to cn, hold to back, k2, p2 from cn.
4-st LPC Sl 2 sts to cn, hold to front, p2, k2, from cn.

YARN (4)

Hat

- 3½oz/100g, 218yd/200m of any worsted weight wool yarn in beige

Mittens

- 218yd/200m, 3½oz/100g of any worsted weight wool yarn in beige

KNITTING NEEDLES

- One pair size 7 (4.5mm) needles *or size to obtain gauge*

ADDITIONAL MATERIALS

- Cable needle (cn)
- Stitch markers
- Tapestry needle

HAT

Cast on 106 sts.
Row 1 K2, *p2, k2; rep from * to end.
Row 2 K the knit sts and p the purl sts.
Rep row 2 until piece measures 3½"/9cm, end with a RS row.
Next row (WS) Work 52 sts in rib as established, [pfb] twice, work in rib to end—108 sts.

Beg chart

Next row (RS) Work 44 sts in rib as established, place marker (pm), work row 1 of chart over 20 sts, pm, work in rib to end. Cont to work chart between markers in this way, sl markers every row, through row 22, then work rows 1–11 once more.

Shape crown

Next (dec) row (WS) [P2, k2tog] 11 times, sl marker, work chart row 12, sl marker, [k2tog, p2] 11 times—86 sts.
Next row (RS) [K2, p1] 11 times, sl marker, work chart row 13, sl marker, [p1, k2] 11 times. Work 2 rows even, working sts outside markers as k the knit sts and p the purl sts.
Next (dec) row (WS) P2, k1, [p1, p3tog, p1, k1] 5 times, sl marker, work chart row 16, sl marker, [k1, p1, p3tog, p1] 5 times, k1, p2—66 sts.
Next row (RS) K2, p1, [k3, p1] 5 times, sl marker, work chart row 17, sl marker, [p1, k3] 5 times, p1, k2. Work 2 rows even.
Next (dec) row (WS) P2, k1, [p1, p2tog, k1] 5 times, sl marker, work chart row 20, sl marker, [k1, p2tog, p1] 5 times, k1, p2—56 sts. Work 2 rows even.
Next (dec) row (RS) [K2, p1] 6 times, [k2, p2tog] twice, 4-st RC, [p2tog, k2] twice, [p1, k2] 6 times—52 sts.
Next (dec) row (WS) [P1, p3tog, p1, k1] 4 times, p4, [k1, p1, p3tog, p1] 4 times—36 sts.
Next row (RS) K the knit sts and p the purl sts.
Next (dec) row (WS) [P3tog, k1] 4 times, p4, [k1, p3tog] 4 times—20 sts.
Next (dec) row (RS) [K2tog] 4 times, 4-st RC, [k2tog] 4 times—12 sts. Cut yarn and draw through rem sts, pull tightly and secure.

Finishing

With RS facing, sew back seam from crown to last 2"/5cm, reverse seam and sew from WS for brim. Fold brim to RS.

Pompom

Make 2½"/6.5cm pompom and secure to top of hat. ■

Right Mitten

Cast on 38 sts.
Row 1 (RS) K2, *p1, k2; rep from * to end.
Row 2 (WS) K the knit sts and p the purl sts. Rep row 2 until piece measures 2¾"/7cm from beg, end with a RS row.
Next (inc) row (WS) P2, [kfb, p2] 12 times—50 sts.
Next row (RS) K2, *p2, k2; rep from * to end. Work 3 rows even in k2, p2 rib as established.

Beg thumb gusset

Next (inc) row (RS) Work 28 sts, place marker (pm), [kfb] twice, pm, work to end—52 sts.

Next row (WS) K the knit sts and p the purl sts.

Next (inc) row (RS) Work 28 sts, sl marker, kfb, k to 1 st before marker, kfb, sl marker, work to end—54 sts.

Next row (WS) K the knit sts and p the purl sts. Rep inc row once more—56 sts.

Next (inc) row (WS) Work 42 sts in pat as established, [pfb] twice, work to end—58 sts.

Beg chart

Note Work chart beg with row 5.

Next row (RS) K2, p2, work row 5 of chart over 20 sts, p2, k2, p2, sl marker, kfb, work to 1 st before marker, kfb, sl marker, work to end. Cont in this way, working thumb inc's every other row until there are 14 sts between markers. Place 14 sts on scrap yarn for thumb.

Next row Work in pats as established, casting on 2 sts at thumb opening—52 sts. Cont to work in pats as established through chart row 22.

Next row (RS) Work 12 sts, 4-st LC, work to end.

Next (dec) row (WS) Work 36 sts, [p2tog] twice, work to end—50 sts. Work even in rib as established until piece measures 8½"/21.5cm from beg, end with a WS row.

Shape top

Next row (RS) K1, pm, ssk, work 20 sts in rib, k2tog, pm, ssk, work 20 sts in rib, k2tog, pm, k1—46 sts.

Paul Amato for Lvarepresents.com

Cables & Ribbing Set

Next row (WS) K the knit sts and p the purl sts.

Next row (RS) K1, sl marker, ssk, work to 2 sts before marker, k2tog, sl marker, ssk, work to 2 sts before marker, k2tog, sl marker, k1—4 sts dec'd.

Next row (WS) K the knit sts and p the purl sts. Rep last 2 rows 4 times more—26 sts. Bind off.

Thumb

Place sts from scrap yarn on needle ready to work a WS row.

Next row (WS) Cast on 1 st, p15.

Next row (RS) Cast on 1 st, k16. Work even in St st (k on RS, p on WS) for 7 rows more.

Next (dec) row (RS) [K2, k2tog] 4 times—12 sts.

Work 1 row even.

Next (dec) row (RS) [K1, k2tog] 4 times—8 sts. Work 1 row even.

Next (dec) row (RS) [K2tog] 4 times—4 sts. Cut yarn and draw through rem sts. Fasten off.

Left Mitten

Work as for right mitten to thumb gusset.

Beg thumb gusset

Next (inc) row (RS) Work 20 sts, pm, [kfb] twice, pm, work to end—52 sts.

Next row (WS) K the knit sts and p the purl sts.

Next (inc) row (RS) Work 20 sts, sl marker, kfb, k to 1 st before marker, kfb, sl marker, work to end—54 sts.

Next row (WS) K the knit sts and p the purl sts. Rep inc row once more—56 sts.

Next (inc) row (WS) Work 12 sts in pat as established, [pfb] twice, work to end—58 sts.

Next row (RS) Work 42 sts in pats as established (including thumb gusset inc's), 4-st LC, work to end—60 sts.

Next row (WS) K the knit sts and p the purl sts.

Beg chart

Note Work chart beg with row 7.

Next row (RS) Work 36 sts in pats as established, including thumb gusset inc's, work chart row 7 over 20 sts, work to end. Cont in this way, working thumb inc's every other row until there are 14 sts between markers. Place 14 sts on scrap yarn for thumb.

Next row Work in pats as established, casting on 2 sts at thumb opening—52 sts. Cont to work in pats as established through chart row 22.

Next row (RS) Work 36 sts in rib, 4-st RC, work to end.

Next (dec) row (WS) Work 12 sts in rib, [p2tog] twice, work to end—50 sts. Complete as for right mitten.

Finishing

Sew top, side and thumb seams. ■

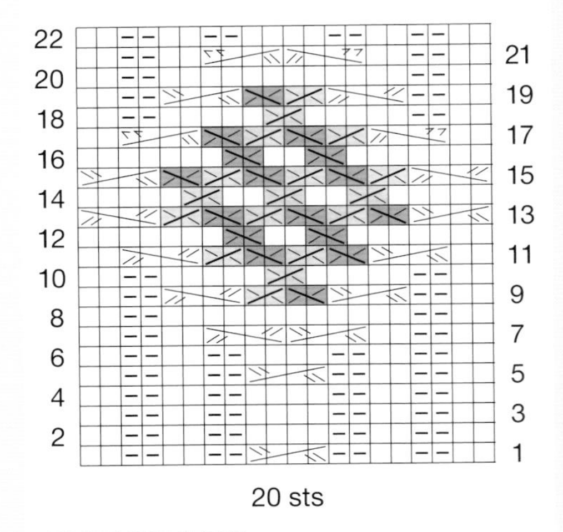

STITCH KEY

- □ k on RS, p on WS
- ⊟ p on RS, k on WS
- 2-st RC
- 2-st LC
- 4-st RC
- 4-st LC
- 4-st RPC
- 4-st LPC

Alpine Ski Set

Measurements

Hat

- **Circumference** 20"/51cm
- **Length excluding earflaps** 9½"/24cm

Mitts

- **Circumference (below thumb)** 7½"/16.5cm
- **Length** 6¾"/17cm

Gauge

22 sts and 30 rows to 4"/10cm over St st using size 6 (4mm) needles.
Take time to check your gauge.

YARN (3)

- 3½oz/100g, 250yd/228m of any DK weight wool in gold (A)
- 125yd/114m, 1¾oz/50g in orange (B), pink (C), and white (D)

KNITTING NEEDLES

- One set (4) size 6 (4mm) double-pointed needles (dpns) *or size to obtain gauge*
- One each sizes 4 and 6 (3.5 and 4mm) circular needles, 16"/40cm long

ADDITIONAL MATERIALS

- Stitch markers
- Stitch holders
- Tapestry needle

Hat

Note Hat is worked from the top down. Change to larger circular needle when there are too many sts to fit on dpn.

With dpn and C, cast on 4 sts.

Row 1 [Kfb] 4 times—8 sts. Divide evenly on 3 needles, join and place marker (pm) for beg of rnd.

Rnd 1 With D, knit.
Rnd 2 With B, [kfb] 8 times—16 sts.
Rnd 3 With B, knit.
Rnd 4 With A, [kfb, k1] 8 times—24 sts.
Rnd 5 With D, knit.
Rnd 6 With C, [kfb, k2] 8 times—32 sts.
Rnd 7 With C, knit.
Rnd 8 With A, [kfb, k3] 8 times—40 sts.
Rnd 9 With D, knit.
Rnd 10 With B, [kfb, k4] 8 times—48 sts.
Rnd 11 With B, knit.
Rnd 12 With A, [kfb, k5] 8 times—56 sts.
Rnd 13 With D, knit.
Rnd 14 With C, [kfb, k6] 8 times—64 sts.
Rnd 15 With C, knit.
Rnd 16 With A, [kfb, k7] 8 times—72 sts.
Rnd 17 With D, knit.
Rnd 18 With B, [kfb, k8] 8 times—80 sts.
Rnd 19 With B, knit.
Rnd 20 With C, knit.
Rnd 21 With D, knit.
Rnd 22 With C, [kfb, k9] 8 times—88 sts.
Rnds 23 and 24 With B, knit.
Rnd 25 With A, knit.
Rnd 26 With D, [kfb, k10] 8 times—96 sts.
Rnds 27 and 28 With C, knit.
Rnd 29 With A, knit.
Rnd 30 With D, [kfb, k11] 8 times—104 sts.
Rnds 31 and 32 With B, knit.
Rnd 33 With C, knit.
Rnd 34 With D, knit.
Rnd 35 With C, knit.
Rnds 36 and 37 With B, knit. With A, k 6 rnds.
Rnd 44 With A, [kfb, k25] 4 times—108 sts.

Beg charts

Work 6-st rep of chart 1, 18 times around.
Cont to work chart in this way through rnd 5.
Next rnd With C, knit.
Next (inc) rnd With C, [kfb, k26] 4 times—112 sts.
Work 8-st rep of chart 2, 14 times around.
Cont to work chart in this way through rnd 7.
Next (dec) rnd With C, [k2tog, k26] 4 times—108 sts.
Next rnd With C, knit. Work 6-st rep of chart 3, 18 times around.
Cont to work chart in this way through rnd 5.
Next rnd With A, [k2tog, k25]—104 sts.
With A, k 2 rnds.

Divide for earflaps

Sl next 12 sts to st holder, rejoin A and k23 for first earflap, sl next 34 sts to 2nd st holder for front of hat, join a 2nd ball of A and k23 for 2nd earflap, sl rem 12 sts to 1st st holder—24 sts on hold for back of hat.
Join A ready to work a WS row on 23 earflap sts. Work 3 rows in St st (p on WS, k on RS).

Next (dec) row (RS) With B, k1, k2tog, k to last 3 sts, ssk, k1—21 sts.
Next row (WS) With B, purl.
Next row With C, rep dec row—19 sts.
Next row With D, purl.
Next row With C, rep dec row—17 sts.
Next row With B, purl.
Next row With B, rep dec row—15 sts.
Next row With D, purl.
Next row With A, rep dec row—13 sts.
Next row With C, purl.
Next row With C, rep dec row—11 sts.
Next row With D, purl.
Next row With A, rep dec row—9 sts.
Next row With B, purl.
Next row With B, rep dec row. Leave rem 7 sts on st holder.
Rep for 2nd earflap.

Finishing

Edging

With RS facing, smaller circular needle and A, k 24 sts from holder for back of hat, *pick up and k 19 sts along side of earflap, k 7 sts from holder for earflap, pick up and k 19 sts along opposite side of earflap*, k 34 sts from holder for front of hat; rep from * to *once more—148 sts. Join and pm for beg of rnd.
Rnd 1 Purl.
Rnd 2 Knit.
Rep last 2 rnds once more. Bind off purlwise.

Cords

Cut three 36"/91.5cm long strands each of A and D. Thread through bottom of earflap creating equal lengths on either side. Twist halves tog tightly into cord, knotting ends.

Pompom

With A and D, make a 3"/7.5cm pompom and sew to top of hat. ■

MITTS

Right Mitt

With smaller dpn and A, cast on 40 sts. Divide evenly on 3 dpns and join, place marker (pm) for beg of rnd.
Rnd 1 With A, *k1, p1; rep from * around. Cont in k1, p1 rib as established in stripes as foll: 2 rnds B, 2 rnds C, 2 rnds D, 2 rnds C, 2 rnds B, 4 rnds A. With A, work 1 rnd more in rib, inc 2 sts evenly around—42 sts. Change to larger dpn. With A, k 4 rnds.

Beg charts

Work 6-st rep of chart 1, 7 times around. Cont to work chart in this way through rnd 5.
Next rnd With C, knit.
Next rnd With C, [k2tog, k19] twice—40 sts. Work 8-st rep of chart 2, 5 times around. Cont to work chart in this way through rnd 7.
Next rnd With C, [kfb, k19] twice—42 sts.

Place thumb

Next rnd With C, k 32. Place last 8 sts worked on st holder, cast on 8 sts, k to end of rnd.
Next rnd Work 6-st rep of row 1 of chart 3 around. Cont to work chart 3 through rnd 5. With A, k 2 rnds. Change to smaller dpn. With A, work 5 rnds in k1, p1 rib. Bind off in pat.

Thumb

With RS facing, larger dpn and C, k8 sts on hold for thumb, then pick up and k 8 sts along thumb opening—16 sts. Divide evenly on dpn and join, pm for beg of rnd. With C, k 6 rnds.
With C, work 2 rnds in k1, p1 rib. Bind off in pat.

Left Mitt

Work as for right mitt to thumb placement.
Next rnd With C, k19. Place last 8 sts worked on st holder, cast on 8 sts, k to end of rnd.
Next rnd Work 6-st rep of rnd 1 of chart 3 around. Complete as for right mitt. ■

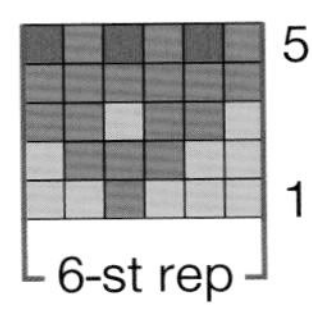

CHART 2

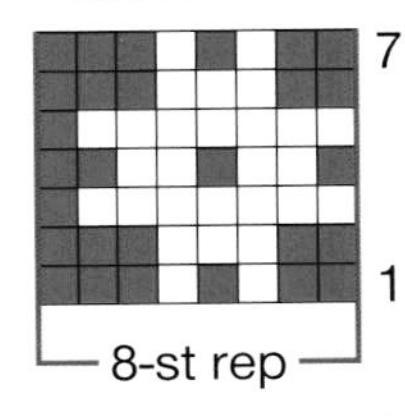

CHART 3

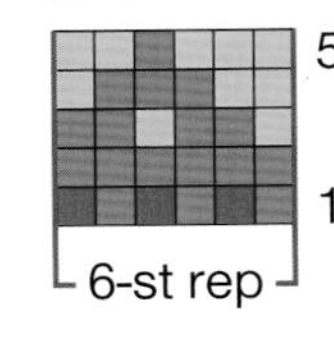

Paul Amato for Lvarepresents.com

Bulky Cabled Beanie & Scarf

Measurements

- **Scarf** 6" x 75"/15.5cm x 190.5cm
- **Hat Circumference** approx 20"/51cm slightly stretched

Gauges

- 24 sts and 19 rows to 4"/10cm over cable pat for scarf using size 10 (6mm) needles.
- 18 sts and 21 rows to 4"/10cm over cable pat for hat using size 10 (6mm) needle.

Take time to check gauges.

Stitch Glossary

4-st RC Sl 2 sts to cn and hold to back, k2, k2 from cn.

4-st LC Sl 2 sts to cn and hold to front, k2, k2 from cn.

6-st RC Sl 3 sts to cn and hold to back, k3, k3 from cn.

6-st LC Sl 3 sts to cn and hold to front, k3, k3 from cn.

Cable Pattern for Scarf

(over 36 sts)

Rows 1 and 5 (RS) [P2, 4-st LC, p2, k6] twice, p2, 4-st LC, p2.

Rows 2, 4 and 6 K the knit sts and p the purl sts.

Row 3 [P2, 4-st LC, p2, 6-st LC] twice, p2, 4-st LC, p2.

Rep rows 1–6 for cable pat for scarf.

Cable Pattern for Hat

(multiple of 18 sts)

Rows 1 and 5 *P2, 4-st RC, p4, k6, p2; rep from * to end.

Rows 2, 4 and 6 K the knit sts and p the purl sts.

Row 3 *P2, 4-st RC, p4, 6-st RC, p2; rep from * to end.

Rep rows 1–6 for cable pat for hat.

YARN (5)

Scarf

- 12oz/339g, 1437yd/384m of any bulky weight wool yarn in gray

Hat

- 958yd/256m, 4oz/226g of any bulky weight wool yarn in gray

KNITTING NEEDLES

- One pair size 10 (6mm) knitting needles *or size to obtain gauge*

ADDITIONAL MATERIALS

- Cable needle
- Tapestry needle

Scarf

Cast on 36 sts. Work in cable pat for scarf until piece measures 75"/190.5cm from beg. Bind off in pat. Block gently to measurements.

Hat

Cast on 90 sts.

Brim

Work rows 1–6 of cable pat for hat (working 18-st rep 5 times) for 17 rows—piece measures approx 3¼"/8cm from beg.

K 1 row on WS for turning ridge.

Note The next row will be a RS row of the crown, but the WS of the brim. Brim will be folded up later.

Crown

Beg with row 1 (RS) of pat, cont in cable pat for hat until piece measures 8"/20.5cm from beg, end with a WS row.

Shape top

Cont in cable pat, working decs as foll:

Dec row 1 (RS) P2, [work 4 sts, p1, p2tog, p1, work 6 sts, p1, p2tog, p1] 4 times, work 4 sts, p1, p2tog, p1, work 6 sts, p2—81 sts. Work 1 row even.

Dec row 2 (RS) P2, [work 4 sts, p1, p2tog, work 6 sts, p1, p2tog] 4 times, work 4 sts, p1, p2tog, work 6 sts, p2—72 sts. Work 1 row even.

Dec row 3 (RS) P2tog, [work 4 sts, p2tog, work 6 sts, p2tog] 4 times, work 4 sts, p2tog, work 6 sts, p2tog—61 sts. Work 1 row even.

Dec row 4 (RS) [P1, k1, k2tog, p2tog, work 6 sts] 5 times, p1—51 sts. Work 1 row even.

Dec row 5 (RS) [K2tog twice, work 6 sts] 5 times, p1—41 sts. Work 1 row even.

Dec row 6 (RS) [K2tog, work 6 sts] 5 times, p1—31 sts. Cut yarn, leaving a 12"/30.5cm end for sewing. Draw yarn through rem sts, gather tog tightly and sew back seam. ■

Shannon Greer for Lvarepresents.com

Rustic Hat & Scarf Set

Measurements

Scarf Approx 7 x 66"/18 x 167.5cm (not including fringe)

Hat

- **Circumference** Approx 21"/53.5cm
- **Length** 8"/20.5cm

Gauge

15 sts and 20 rows to 4"/10cm over St st using size 9 (5.5mm) needles with MC held double.

Take time to check your gauge.

Note MC is held double throughout. CC is used single stranded.

Pattern Stitch 1

Rows 1–3 With MC, knit.

Row 4 (WS) P1, *yo, p2tog; rep from * to end.

Rows 5 and 6 Knit.

Rows 7–10 With CC, k on RS, p on WS.

Rep rows 1–10 for pat st 1.

Pattern Stitch 2

Rows 1–3 With MC, Knit.

Row 4 (WS) P1, *yo, p2tog; rep from * to end.

Rows 5 and 6 Knit.

Rows 7–10 With MC, k on RS, p on WS.

Rep rows 1–10 for pat st 2.

Scarf

With MC and size 9 needles, cast on 29 sts. Work 3 reps of pat st 1. Cut CC.

Beg pat st 2

Work in pat st 2 for 28 reps. Work pat st 1 three times and rows 1–6 once more. Bind off.

YARN (4) (2)

- 10½oz/300m, 1020yd/930m of any worsted weight wool/cotton yarn gray multi (MC)
- 128yd/117m, 1¾oz/50m of any sport weight wool yarn orange (CC)

KNITTING NEEDLES

- One pair size 9 (5.5mm) needles *or size to obtain gauge*
- One size 9 (5.5mm) circular needle 16"/40cm long
- One set (5) size 9 (5.5mm) double-pointed needles (dpns)

ADDITIONAL MATERIALS

- Size I-9 (5.5mm) crochet hook
- Tapestry needle

Finishing

Fringe

Note Make 9 for each end of scarf.

Cut ten 8"/20.5cm strands of CC. Holding 10 strands tog, fold in half making loop. With crochet hook, draw loop through st on cast-on or bound-off edge. Pull ends through loop. Tighten.

Hat

With circular needle and MC, cast on 79 sts. Do not join. Work 1 rep of pat st 1. Work rows 1–6 once more. PM and join into round. Cont with MC and work in St st until piece measures 6½"/16.5cm from beg.

Shape crown

Note Change to dpns when sts no longer fit comfortably on circular needle.

Next rnd *K2tog; rep from * to last st, k1—40 sts.

Knit one rnd.

Rep last 2 rnds 3 times more—5 sts. Cut yarn and thread through rem sts.

Finishing

Sew seam. ■

Shannon Greer for Lvarepresents.com

Capelet & Beret

Measurements

Beret

- **Diameter** approx 10"/25.5cm

Capelet

- **Width at lower edge (buttoned)** approx 60"/152cm
- **Length from center back neck (without collar)** 11¼"/28.5cm

Gauges

Beret

12 sts and 20 rnds to 4"/10cm over k3, p3 rib using size 10 (6mm) needles.

Capelet

16 sts and 20 rows to 4"/10cm over k3, p2 rib using size 10 (6mm) needles.
Take time to check your gauges.

K3, P2 Rib

(over a multiple of 5 sts plus 2)
Row 1 (RS) P2, *k3, p2; rep from * to end.
Row 2 K2, *p3, k2; rep from * to end. Rep rows 1 and 2 for k3, p2 rib.

Decrease Wedge

(over 7 sts)
Row 1 (RS) P2, k3, p2.
Row 2 K2, p3, k2.
Dec row 3 P2, SK2P, p2—5 sts.
Row 4 K2, p1, k2.
Dec row 5 P1, p2tog, p2—4 sts.
Row 6 K4.
Dec row 7 P1, p3tog—2 sts.
Row 8 P2.
Note The decrease wedge rows 3–7 are worked over the designated ribs at intervals for wedge shape decreasing. The other rows are given for clarity.

Beret

YARN (5)
- 3½oz/100g, 120yd/110m of any bulky weight wool tweed yarn in fuchsia

KNITTING NEEDLES
- One set (5) size 10 (6mm) double-pointed needles (dpns) *or size to obtain gauge*

ADDITIONAL MATERIALS
- Size I/9 (5.5mm) crochet hook

Capelet

YARN (5)
- 12¼oz/350g, 420yd/385m of any bulky weight wool tweed yarn in fuchsia

KNITTING NEEDLES
- Size 10 (6mm) circular needle, 36"/90cm long *or size to obtain gauge*
- One pair size 10 (6mm) needles

ADDITIONAL MATERIALS
- Five 1⅛"/27mm buttons
- Stitch markers
- Stitch holders
- Tapestry needle

Sloped Cast On

On the row previous to the cast-on, sl the last st wyib on RS, wyif on WS; then at beg of next cast-on row, use cable cast-on method with two needles.

Beret

Beg at center, with crochet hook, ch 4, join with sl st to first ch to form ring. Ch 1, work 11 sc in ring.

Rnd 1 With loop on hook, pick up 3 more loops in the next 3 sc and sl from end of hook to first dpn; then pick up 4 loops and sl to 2nd dpn; pick up 4 more loops and sl to 3rd dpn—12 sts with 4 sts on each dpn. Weave in a contrast yarn to carry along and mark the beg of rnds.
Rnd 2 Needle 1: [kfb, pfb] twice; Needle 2: [kfb, pfb] twice; Needle 3: [kfb, pfb] twice—24 sts.
Rnds 3 and 4 [K2, p2] 6 times.
Rnd 5 Needle 1: [k2, pfb, p1] twice; Needle 2: [k2, pfb, p1] twice; Needle 3: [k2, pfb, p1] twice—30 sts.
Rnd 6 [K2, p3] 6 times.
Rnd 7 Needle 1: [k2, p1, pfb, p1] twice; Needles 2 and 3: work same as Needle 1—36 sts.
Rnd 8 [K2, p4] 6 times.
Rnd 9 Needle 1: *k2, p1, (p1, k1) into next st, p2*; rep between*'s once more; Needles 2 and 3: work same as Needle 1—42 sts.
Rnd 10 [K2, p2, k1, p2] 6 times.
Rnd 11 Needle 1: *k2, p2, M1, k1, M1, p2*; rep between *'s once more; Needles 2 and 3: work same as Needle 1—54 sts.
Rnd 12 [K2, p2, k3, p2] 6 times.
Rnd 13 Needle 1: *kfb, k1, p2, k3, p2*; rep between *'s once more; Needles 2 and 3: work same as Needle 1—60 sts.
Rnd 14 [K3, p2] 12 times.
Rnd 15 Needle 1: *k3, pfb, p1, k3, p2*; rep between *'s once more; Needles 2 and 3: work same as Needle 1—66 sts.
Rnd 16 [K3, p3, k3, p2] 6 times.
Rnd 17 Needle 1: *k3, p3, k3, pfb, p1*; rep between *'s once more; Needles 2 and 3: work same as Needle 1—72 sts.
Rnd 18 *K3, p3; rep from * around. At this

Paul Amato for Lvarepresents.com

Capelet & Beret

point, divide sts onto 4 needles with 18 sts on each needle and cont to work in rnds of k3, p3 rib for 18 rnds more. Bind off knitwise. Do not fasten off. Turn hat to the WS and with loop on hook, ch 1, and working into front loops of the bound-off edge only, *work 2 hdc, skip 1 st; rep from * around, join and fasten off.

Note Adjust the number of hdc for the desired head circumference.

Finishing

Immerse hat in cold water and roll in a towel to squeeze out excess moisture. Then insert a 10"/25.5cm dinner plate into hat and leave to dry to form the beret shape.

Capelet

Back Segment

With size 10 (6mm) straight needles, cast on 47 sts.

Row 1 (RS) P2, [k3, p2] 9 times.

Row 2 (WS) Cast on 5 sts, k2, *p3, k2; rep from * to end—52 sts.

Row 3 (RS) Cast on 5 sts, p2, *k3, p2; rep from * to end—57 sts.

Rows 4, 6 and 8 Rep row 2.

Rows 5, 7 and 9 Rep row 3—87 sts.

Turn to WS, cast on 15 sts and leave 102 sts on hold on the circular needle.

Left Front Segment

With size 10 (6mm) straight needles, cast on 32 sts.

Row 1 (WS) P3, [k1, p1] twice, k1, p2, [k2, p3] 4 times, k2.

Row 2 (RS) Cast on 5 sts, p2, [k3, p2] 5 times, sl 2 wyib, [p1, k1] twice, p1, sl 3 wyib—37 sts.

Row 3 (WS) P3, [k1, p1] twice, k1, p2 (10-st band); k2, *p3, k2; rep from * to end.
Row 4 (RS) Cast on 5 sts, *p2, k3; rep from * to 2 sts before band, p2, work sl 2 wyib, [p1, k1] twice, p1, sl 3 wyib—42 sts.
Rows 5 and 7 Rep row 3.
Row 6 Rep row 4—47 sts.
Row 8 Rep row 4—52 sts.
Row 9 Rep row 3.
Turn to the RS and cast on 13 sts, cut yarn and pm, then sl these 65 sts to left end of the circular needle with the marker between front and back sts.

Right Front

With size 10 (6mm) straight needles, cast on 32 sts.
Row 1 (RS) Sl 3 wyib, p1, [k1, p1] twice, sl 2 wyib; p2, [k3, p2] 5 times.
Row 2 (WS) Cast on 5 sts, *k2, p3; rep from * to last 2 sts before band (from Left Front Segment, row 3), k2, p2, k1, [p1, k1] twice, p3—37 sts.
Row 3 Sl 3 wyib, p1, [k1, p1] twice, sl 2 wyib; work in rib to end.
Row 4 Rep row 2—42 sts.
Row 5 Rep row 3.
Row 6 Rep row 2—47 sts.
Buttonhole row 7 (RS) Sl 3 wyib, p1, k1, (yo) twice, k2tog (for vertical buttonhole row 1), work even to end.
Buttonhole row 8 Cast on 5 sts, *k2, p3; rep from * to 2 sts before band, k2, p2, k1, p1, sl the double yo, yo twice again (for buttonhole row 2), work to end.
Buttonhole row 9 Sl 3, p1, k1, k1 through the yo's (buttonhole row 3), work to end—52 sts.
Turn and cast on 13 sts at beg of next row, then place marker. Cast on 15 more sts (for back). Sl these 80 sts to circular needle in position for right front.
Cut yarn.

Capelet

Rejoin yarn from the RS and work as foll:
Row 1 (RS) Work 65 sts of right front, sl marker, work 117 sts of back, sl marker, work 65 sts of left front—247 sts.
Row 2 Work even.
Row 3 Work 20 sts, work dec wedge row 3 over next 7 sts, work to 4 sts before marker, *k2tog, place new marker, k1, SKP removing previous marker*; work 34 sts, work dec wedge row 3 over 7 sts, work 33 sts, work dec wedge row 3 over next 7 sts, work to 1 st before marker; rep between *'s once, work 34 sts, work dec wedge row 3 over 7 sts, work 20 sts—235 sts.
Row 4 Work even, working wedge row 4 over the 4 dec'd segments.
Row 5 Work even, working wedge row 5 over the 4 dec'd segments—231 sts.
Row 6 Work even, working wedge row 6 over the 4 dec'd segments.
Row 7 Work row 7 of the dec wedge over the 4 dec'd segments AND work the side dec's as foll: *work to 2 sts before marker, k2tog, sl marker, k1, SKP; rep from * once more, work to end—219 sts.
Row 8 Work even.
Row 9 Work 25 sts, *work dec wedge row 3 over next 7 sts*, work to first marker, sl marker, work 25 sts; rep between *'s once, work 43 sts; rep between *'s once, work to 2nd marker, sl marker, work 25 sts; rep between *'s once, work 25 sts—211 sts.
Row 10 Work even, working wedge row 4 over the 4 dec'd segments.
Row 11 Working row 5 of the dec wedge over the 4 dec'd segments, work the side dec's as foll: *work to 2 sts before marker, k2tog, sl marker, k1, SKP; rep from * once more, work to end—203 sts.
Row 12 Work even, working wedge row 6 over the 4 dec'd segments.
Row 13 Work in pat, working wedge row 7 over the 4 dec'd segments—195 sts.
Row 14 Work even.
Buttonhole row 15 Sl 3, p1, k1, (yo) twice, k2tog, work 23 sts in pat, *work dec wedge row 3 over the next 7 sts*; work to 2 sts before marker, k2tog, sl marker, k1, SKP, work 11 sts; rep between *'s, work 53 sts in pat; rep between *'s, work 11 sts, k2tog, sl marker, k1, SKP, work 11 sts; rep between *'s, work to end—183 sts.
Row 16 Work in pat, working wedge row 4 over the 4 dec'd segments AND work buttonhole row 2 at end of row.
Row 17 Work in pat working wedge row 5 over the 4 dec'd segments AND work buttonhole row 3 at beg of row—179 sts.
Row 18 Rep row 12.
Row 19 Work in pat working wedge row 7 over the 4 dec'd segments and dec 2 sts at markers as before—167 sts.
Row 20 Work even.
Row 21 Work 20 sts, *work dec wedge row 3 over next 7 sts*, work 33 sts; rep between *'s once, work 33 sts; rep between *'s once, work 33 sts; rep between *'s once, work 20 sts—159 sts.
Row 22 Rep row 10.
Row 23 Rep row 11—151 sts.
Row 24 Rep row 12.
Row 25 Rep row 13—143 sts.

Row 26 Work even.
Row 27 Work to 2 sts before marker, k2tog, sl marker, k1, SKP, work 3 sts, *work dec wedge row 3 over next 7 sts*, work 43 sts; rep between *'s once, work 3 sts, k2tog, sl marker, k1, SKP, work to end—135 sts.
Row 28 Work even, working wedge row 4 over the 2 dec'd wedges.
Row 29 Work even, working wedge row 5 over the 2 dec'd segments—133 sts.
Row 30 Work even, working wedge row 6 over the 2 dec'd segments.
Buttonhole row 31 Sl 3, p1, k1, (yo) twice, k2tog, *work to 2 sts before marker, k2tog, sl marker, k1, SKP*, work wedge row 7 over the 2 dec'd segments; rep between *'s once, work to end—125 sts.
Row 32 Work even, working buttonhole row 2 at end of the row. There are 35 sts in right front, 54 sts between markers for back and 36 sts in left front.
Row 33 Work buttonhole row 3 at beg of row, work to marker, sl marker, work 9 sts, *work wedge dec row 3 over next 7 sts*, work 23 sts; rep between *'s once, work to end—121 sts.
Row 34 Work even, working wedge row 4 over the 2 dec'd segments.

Shape Neck

Row 35 (RS) Work 10 sts and sl to a st holder, *work to 2 sts before marker, k2tog, sl marker, k1, SKP*, work wedge row 5 over the 2 dec'd segments; rep between *'s once, work to the last 10 sts, sl these sts to holder—95 sts.
Row 36 (WS) Bind off 3 sts, work even to end, working wedge row 6 over the 2 dec'd segments.
Row 37 (RS) Bind off 3 sts, *work to 2 sts before marker, k2tog, sl marker, k1, SKP*; work wedge row 7 over the 2 dec'd segments; rep between *'s once more, work to end—81 sts.
Row 38 Bind off 3 sts, work even to end.
Row 39 Bind off 3 sts, *work to 2 sts before marker, k2tog, sl marker, k1, SKP*; rep between *'s once, work even to end—71 sts.
Rows 40–45 Rep rows 38 and 39 for 3 times—41 sts.
Row 46 Work even.
Row 47 Dec 2 sts at each marker—37 sts. Cut yarn.

Collar

Row 1 (RS) From the RS, sl the first 10 sts to needle, rejoin yarn and pick up and k 15 sts along the shaped collar edge, rib 37 sts from needle, pick up and k 15 sts along the shaped collar, work the 10 sts from holder—87 sts. Cont with established 10 sts for front bands, work 11 rows more in rib.
Next 3 rows Work buttonhole rows 1–3 over the first 10-st band. Work 13 rows even.
Next 3 rows Work buttonhole rows 1–3 over the first 10-st band. Work 3 rows even. Bind off.

Lower Edge

From RS, pick up and k 1 st in each st along lower edge.
Bind off knitwise.

Finishing

Block to measurements. Sew on buttons. ■

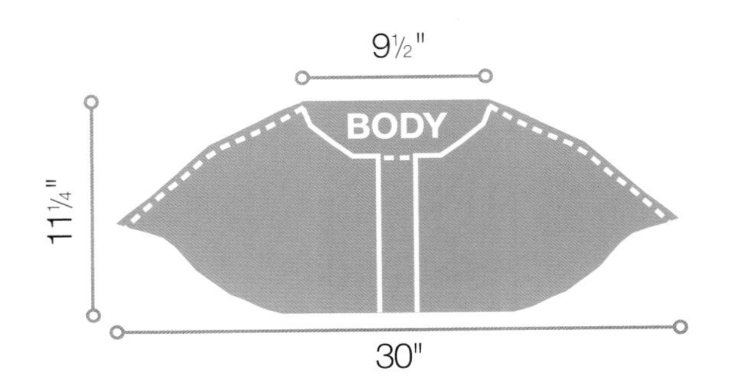

Leaf Hat & Mittens

Sizes
Hat and mittens sized for Adult Woman.

Measurements
Hat
- **Circumference** 20"/51cm (stretched)
- **Length** 9"/23cm

Mittens
- **Hand circumference** 7"/18cm
- **Length** 11½"/29cm

Gauge
14 sts and 20 rnds to 4"/10cm over St st using larger needles.
Take time to check your gauge.

Hat

YARN (5)
- 3½oz/100g, 110yd/101m of any bulky weight variegated wool

KNITTING NEEDLES
- One each sizes 9 and 10½ (5.5 and 6.5mm) circular needles, 24"/60cm long *or size to obtain gauge*
- One set (5) size 10½ (6.5) double-pointed needles (dpns)

Mittens

YARN (5)
- 3½oz/100g, 110yd/101m of any bulky weight variegated wool

KNITTING NEEDLES
- One set (5) each size 9 and 10½ (5.5 and 6.5) double-pointed needles (dpns) *or size to obtain gauge*

ADDITIONAL MATERIALS
- Stitch markers
- Scrap yarn or stitch holder
- Tapestry needle

Hat
With smaller circular needle, cast on 76 sts. Join, taking care not to twist sts. Place marker (pm) for beg of rnd and slip marker every rnd.
Next (rib) rnd *[K1, p2] 6 times, k1; rep from * three times more.
Rep rib rnd until piece measures 2"/5cm from beg.
Change to larger circular needle.
Next (set-up) rnd [K7, pm, p2, k1, p2, pm, k7] 4 times.

Beg Chart
Note Stitch count changes in chart rnds.
Next rnd [K to marker, sl marker, work chart rnd 1, sl marker] 4 times, work to end of rnd. Cont to work chart in this manner through rnd 8. Rep rnds 1–8 once more, then rnds 1–5 once—84 sts in rnd.

Shape Crown
Note Change to dpn when sts no longer fit on circular needle.
Rnd 1 (dec) [K6, ssk, p1, k3, p1, k2tog, k6] 4 times—76 sts.
Rnd 2 (dec) [K7, p1, S2KP, p1, k7] 4 times—68 sts.
Rnd 3 (dec) [K6, ssk, k1, k2tog, k6] 4 times—60 sts.
Rnd 4 Knit.
Rnd 5 (dec) [K6, S2KP, k6] 4 times—52 sts.
Rnd 6 Knit.
Rnd 7 (dec) [K5, S2KP, k5] 4 times—44 sts.
Rnd 8 Knit.
Rnd 9 (dec) [K4, S2KP, k4] 4 times—36 sts.
Rnd 10 Knit.
Rnd 11 (dec) [K3, S2KP, k3] 4 times—28 sts.
Rnd 12 Knit.
Rnd 13 (dec) [K2, S2KP, k2] 4 times—20 sts.
Rnd 14 Knit.
Rnd 15 (dec) [K2tog] to end—10 sts.
Cut yarn and draw through rem sts.

Mittens (make 2)
Cuff
With smaller dpn, cast on 26 sts.
Join, taking care not to twist sts. Place marker (pm) for beg of rnd and slip marker every rnd.
Next (rib) rnd *[K1, p2] 4 times, k1; rep from * once more.

Leaf Hat & Mittens

Rep rib rnd until cuff measures 3"/7.5cm from beg. Change to larger needles.

Begin Chart

Note Stitch count changes in chart rnds.

Next (set-up) rnd [K4, pm, p2, k1, p2, pm, k4] twice.

Next rnd [K to marker, sl marker, work chart rnd 1, sl marker] twice, k to end of rnd.

Cont to work chart in this manner through rnd 8.

Thumb Gusset

Next (inc) rnd Work in pat as established over 13 sts, pm for gusset, M1, pm for gusset, work to end of rnd.

Work 1 rnd even, slipping markers.

Next (inc) rnd Work to first gusset marker, sl marker, M1, k to next gusset marker, M1, sl marker, work to end of round.

Work 1 rnd even, slipping markers.

Next (inc) rnd Work to first gusset marker, sl marker, M1, k to next gusset marker M1, sl marker, work to end of round.

Work 1 rnd even.

Rep last 2 rnds twice more—7 sts between gusset markers.

Hand

Next rnd Cont in pat as established to gusset marker, place next 7 sts on scrap yarn or stitch holder for thumb, removing markers, work in pat to end of rnd.

Cont in pat until rnd 8 of chart has been completed 4 times—26 sts in rnd.

Rep rnds 1–5 once more—30 sts.

Shape Mitten Top

Rnd 1 (dec) [K3, ssk, p1, k3, p1, k2tog, k3] twice—26 sts.

Rnd 2 (dec) [K4, p1, S2KP, p1, k4] twice—22 sts.

Rnd 3 (dec) [K3, ssk, k1, k2tog, k3] twice—18 sts.

Rnd 4 Knit.

Rnd 5 (dec) [K3, S2KP, k3] twice—14 sts.

Rnd 6 Knit.

Rnd 7 (dec) [K2, S2KP, k2] twice—10 sts.

Rnd 8 (dec) [Ssk, k1, k2tog] twice—6 sts.

Cut yarn and thread through rem sts.

Fasten off.

Thumb

With larger dpn, pick up and k 5 sts along top of thumb opening, place thumb sts onto larger dpn—12 sts.

Distribute evenly on 3 dpns1. Work in St st (k every rnd) until thumb is ½"/1.5cm shorter than desired thumb length.

Next (dec) rnd [K2tog] 6 times—6 sts.

Next rnd Knit.

Next (dec) rnd [K2tog] 3 times—3 sts.

Cut yarn and thread through rem sts.

Fasten off. ■

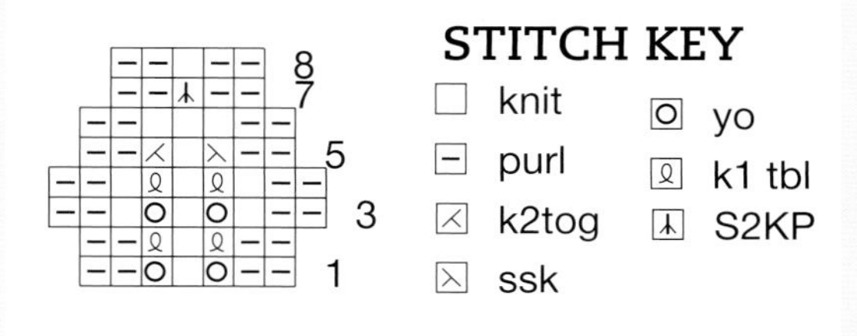

Paul Amato for LVArepresents.com

Beaded Beanie & Scarf

Measurements

Hat

- **Head circumference** 19"/48cm
- **Length** 9"/23cm

Scarf Approx 5½x 65"/14 x 165cm

Gauge

15 sts and 25 rows to 4"/10cm over St st using size 10 (6mm) needles and one strand each of A and B held tog.

Take time to check your gauge.

Stitch Glossary

PB (place bead) Push pre-strung bead up to front of work snug against last st worked and knit or purl, drawing bead through st being worked.

pfb Purl into front and back of st for an inc 1.

YARN 4

- 1¾oz/50g, 450yd/412m of any worsted weight wool/cotton yarn in soft teal (A)
- 5¼oz/150g, 411yd/375m of any worsted weight wool/cotton yarn in blue (B)

KNITTING NEEDLE

- One pair size 10 (6mm) needles *or size to obtain gauge*

ADDITIONAL MATERIALS

- 300 size 3–4mm glass E beads in brass—60 for hat, 240 for scarf
- Sewing needle to fit through bead opening
- Stitch markers
- Tapestry needle

Notes

1 Hat and scarf are worked with one strand each of A and B held tog throughout.

2 Beads are pre-strung on A and placed when instructed.

3 Hat is worked from side to side with short-row shaping. Crown is picked up and knit along short-row edge. Ribbing is picked up along unshaped edge. Purl side of hat is RS.

Hat

With sewing needle, thread 60 beads on A.

With one strand each of A and B held tog, cast on 29 sts.

Row 1 (WS) Knit.

Row 2 P9, PB, p9, PB, p9.

Row 3 Knit.

Row 4 short row P17, turn.

Row 5 short row Knit to end of row—mark this edge.

Row 6 P4, PB, [p9, PB] twice, p4.

Row 7 Knit.

Row 8 Purl.

Rep rows 1–8 until piece measures 19"/48cm from beg along marked edge, end with a row 7.

Bind off 28 sts. Do not fasten off—1 st rem on needle

Crown

With RS facing and last st on needle, pick up and k 39 sts evenly along unmarked edge of hat—40 sts.

Next row (WS) Knit.

Next (dec) row *P2 tog; rep from * to end—20 sts rem.

Rep dec row once more—10 sts rem.

Cut yarn leaving long tail. Thread yarn through rem sts and draw tight.

Ribbing

With RS facing, pick up and k 58 sts evenly along marked edge of hat.

Row 1 (WS) P2, * k2, p2; rep from * across.

Row 2 K2, *p2, k2; rep from * across.

Rep rows 1 and 2 once more and row 1 once.

Bind off loosely in pat. Cut yarn leaving a long tail for sewing. Sew seam.

Scarf

With sewing needle, thread 50 beads on A.

With one strand each of A and B held tog, cast on 304 sts.

Ribbed Edge

Rows 1–6 *K2, p2; rep from * across.

Next (dec) row (RS) K1, k2 tog, [k3, k2 tog] 60 times, k1—243 sts rem.

Knit 1 row.

Beaded Section

Note When 50 beads have been placed, break A, thread 50 beads more and rejoin A. Repeat as needed.

Row 1 (RS) P5, pm, k to last 5 sts, pm, p5.

Row 2 K5, sl marker (sm), p to 2nd marker, sm, k5. Cont to slip markers every row.

Row 3 K6, [PB, k9] 23 times, PB, k6.

Row 4 P6, [PB, p9] 23 times, PB, p6.

Row 5 Knit.

Row 6 Rep Row 2.

Row 7 P5, k6, [PB, k9] 22 times, PB, k6, p5.

Row 8 K5, p6, [PB, p9] 22 times, PB, p6, k5.

Row 9 Knit.

Row 10 Purl.

Row 11 Rep Row 3.

Row 12 K5, p1, [PB, p9] 23 times, PB, p1, k5.

Row 13 Rep row 1, slipping markers.

Row 14 Rep row 2.

Row 15 K11, [PB, k9] 22 times, PB, k11.
Row 16 P11, [PB, p9] 22 times, PB, p11.
Row 17 Knit.
Row 18 Rep Row 2.
Row 19 P5, k1, [PB, k9] 23 times, PB, k1, p5.
Row 20 Rep Row 12.
Row 21 Knit.
Row 22 Purl.

Ribbed Edge

Next row (RS) Purl 1 row.
Next (inc) row (WS) P1, pfb, [k3, pfb] 60 times, p1—304 sts.
Next 6 rows *K2, p2; rep from * across.
Bind off in pat. ■

Double Seed Stitch Hat & Cowl

Sizes

Hat One Size

Cowl Small, Medium, Large, X-Large. Shown in size Small.

Measurements

Hat

- **Head circumference** 20½"/52cm
- **Length** 7"/18cm

Cowl

- **Width at lower edge** 38 (43, 48, 53)"/96.5 (109, 122, 134.5)cm
- **Length (without neck edge rolled)** 16 (16½, 17, 17½)"/40.5 (41.5, 43, 44.5)cm

Gauge

16 sts and 18 rows to 4"/10cm over double seed st using size 10 (6mm) and one strand each of A and B held tog.

Take time to check your gauge.

Double Seed Stitch

(over an even number of sts)

Row 1 (RS) *K1, p1; rep from * to end.

Row 2 K the knit sts and p the purl sts.

Row 3 *P1, k1; rep from * to end.

Row 4 K the knit sts and p the purl sts.

Rep rows 1–4 for double seed st.

Hat

Brim

With straight needles and one strand each of A and B held tog, cast on 16 sts. Work in double seed st until piece measures 20½"/52cm from beg. Bind off. Sew cast-on edge to bound-off edge.

Hat

YARN (4)

- 1¾oz/50g, 120yd/110m of any worsted weight wool tweed in golden green (A)
- 1¾oz/50g, 225yd/206m of any worsted weight mohair blend in olive (B)

KNITTING NEEDLES

- One pair size 10 (6mm) needles *or size to obtain gauge*
- One set (5) size 10 (6mm) double-pointed needles (dpns)

Cowl

YARN (4)

- 5¼oz/150g, 360yd/330m (7oz/200g, 480yd/440m; 7oz/200g, 480yd/440m; 8¾oz/250g, 600yd/550m) of any worsted weight wool tweed in golden green (A)
- 3½oz/100g, 450yd/412m (5¼oz/150g, 675yd/618m; 5¼oz/150g, 675yd/618m; 7oz/200g, 900yd/824m) of any worsted weight mohair blend in olive (B)

KNITTING NEEDLES

- One pair size 10 (6mm) needles *or size to obtain gauge*
- One size 10 (6mm) circular needle, 24"/60cm long

ADDITIONAL MATERIALS

- Stitch markers
- Tapestry needle

Crown

With RS facing, dpn and one strand each of A and B held tog, pick up and k 80 sts along one long edge of brim. Divide sts evenly over 4 dpn—20 sts on each needle. Place marker for beg of rnd. Knit 1 rnd.

Dec rnd [Ssk, k to last 2 sts on needle, k2tog] 4 times—2 sts dec'd on each dpn, 8 sts dec'd in total.

Rep dec rnd every other rnd 8 times more—2 sts rem on each dpn, 8 sts in rnd.

Cut yarn, leaving long tail. Thread tail through rem sts.

Cowl

Body

With straight needles and one strand each of A and B held tog, cast on 28 (28, 30, 30) sts. Work in double seed st for 38 (43, 48, 53)"/96.5 (109, 122, 134.5)cm. Bind off. Sew cast-on edge to bound-off edge for center back seam.

Yoke

With RS facing, circular needle and one strand each of A and B held tog, beg at center back seam, pick up and k 152 (172, 192, 212) sts evenly along edge of body. Place marker (pm) for beg of rnd.

Next rnd K30 (35, 40, 45), pm, k16, pm, k60 (70, 80, 90), pm, k16, pm, k 30 (35, 40, 45).

Next (dec) rnd [K to 2 sts before next marker, k2tog, sl marker, ssk] 4 times, k to end of rnd—144 (164, 184, 204) sts.

Cont in St st (k every rnd), rep dec rnd every other rnd 4 (6, 8, 10) times more—112 (116, 120, 124) sts. Work even until yoke measures 9 (9½, 9½, 10)"/23 (24, 24, 25.5)cm from picked-up rnd. Bind off loosely. ■

Paul Amato for LVArepresents.com

Colorwork & Garter Stitch Set

Measurements

Scarf

- 9" x 87"/22.5cm x 217.5cm

Hat

- **Circumference** 22"/56cm

Gauge

Scarf

18 sts and 21 rows to 4"/10cm over St st using straight needles.

Hat

18 sts and 22 rows to 4"/10cm over St st in the round using dpns.

Take time to check your gauge.

YARN (4)

- 15¾oz/450g, 585yd/540m of any aran weight wool in navy (MC)
- 3½oz/100g, 130yd/120m in natural (CC)

KNITTING NEEDLES

- Size 8 (5mm) needles *or size to obtain gauge*
- Size 8 (5mm) double-pointed needles (dpns)

ADDITIONAL MATERIALS

- Stitch holder
- Tapestry needle

Note

When changing colors, twist yarns on WS to prevent holes in work.

Scarf

Scarf first half

With CC and straight needles, cast on 41 sts. Work in garter st for 8 rows, then work next 52 rows of scarf from text or scarf chart.

Rows 1–4 With MC, work in St st.
Row 5 (RS) With CC, *sl 1, k1; rep from * to last st, end sl 1.
Rows 6–8 Work in St st.
Row 9 With MC, *sl 1, k1; rep from * to last st, end sl 1.
Rows 10–12 Work in St st.
Row 13 With CC, *sl 1, k1; rep from * to last st, end sl 1.
Row 14 Purl.
Row 15 *K1 CC, k1 MC; rep from * to last st, end k1 CC.
Row 16 With MC, purl.
Rows 17–19 Work in St st.
Rows 20 and 26 *P1 CC, p2 MC; rep from * to last 2 sts, end p1 CC, p1 MC.
Rows 21 and 25 *K2 MC, k1 CC; rep from * to last 2 sts, end k2 MC.
Rows 22 and 24 P1 MC, *p1 CC, p2 MC; rep from * to last st, end p1 CC.
Row 23 With CC, knit.
Rep rows 1–26 once more.
With MC, work even in St st until piece measures 42"/106.5cm from beg, ending with a RS row. Place sts on holder.

Scarf second half

Make as for Scarf First Half, ending with a WS row.

Finishing

With RS facing up, lay 2 scarf halves tog at holders. Graft together with Kitchener St.

Hat

Brim

With CC and dpns, cast on 96 sts. Place marker and join for knitting in the round, taking care not to twist sts. Work in garter st for 9 rnds, then work next 23 rnds of hat from text or hat chart.

Rnds 1–4 With MC, knit.
Rnd 5 With CC, *sl 1, k1; rep from * to marker.
Rnds 6–8 Knit.
Rnd 9 With MC, *sl 1, k1; rep from * to marker.
Rnds 10–12 Knit.
Rnd 13 With CC, *sl 1, k1; rep from * to marker.
Rnd 14 Knit.
Rnd 15 *K1 CC, k1 MC; rep from * to marker.
Rnds 16–19 With MC, knit.
Rnd 20 *K1 CC, k2 MC; rep from * to marker.
Rnd 21 K1 MC, *k1 CC, k2 MC; rep from * to last st, end k1 MC.
Rnd 22 *K2 MC, k1 CC; rep from * to marker.
Rnd 23 With CC, knit.
With MC, knit 2 rnds.

Crown shaping

Rnd 1 *K10, k2tog; rep from * to marker—88 sts.
Rnds 2–3 Knit.
Rnd 4 *K9, k2tog; rep from * to marker—80 sts.
Rnds 5–6 Knit.
Rnd 7 *K8, k2tog; rep from * to marker—72 sts.
Rnds 8–9 Knit.
Rnd 10 *K7, k2tog; rep from * to marker—64 sts.
Rnds 11, 13, 15, 17, and 19 Knit.
Rnd 12 *K6, k2tog; rep from * to marker—56 sts.

Rnd 14 *K5, k2tog; rep from * to marker—48 sts.

Rnd 16 *K4, k2tog; rep from * to marker—40 sts.

Rnd 18 *K3, k2tog; rep from * to marker—32 sts.

Rnd 20 *K2, k2tog; rep from * to marker—24 sts.

Rnd 21 *K1, k2tog; rep from * to marker—16 sts.

Rnd 22 *K2tog; rep from * to marker—8 sts. Cut 12"/30.5cm tail, thread through rem sts and cinch tightly to close. ■

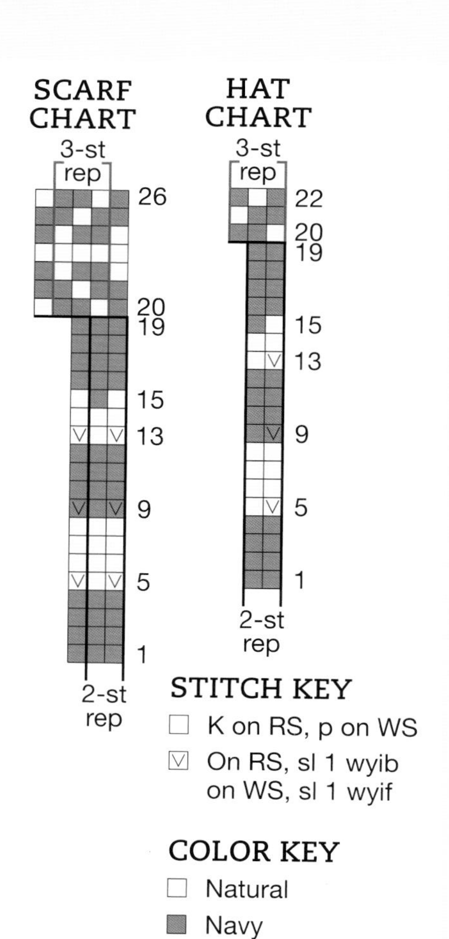

Jenny Acheson

Slip Stitch Set

Measurements

Scarf

- **Width** approx 14"/35.5cm
- **Length** 78"/198cm

Cap

Sized for Small (Medium/Large).
Shown in size Medium/Large.

- **Brim circumference** 19¾ (22)"/50 (56)cm (unstretched)
- **Length** 8½ (9)"/21.5 (23)cm

Gauges

Scarf

33 sts and 32 rows to 4"/10cm over slip st rib, laid flat without stretching, using size 8 (5mm) needles.

Cap

13 sts and 20 rnds to 4"/10cm over brioche rib, slightly stretched, using size 7 (4.5mm) needles.

Take time to check your gauges.

Slip Stitch Rib

(multiple of 4 sts plus 3)

Row 1 (RS) *K3, bring yarn to front between needles, sl 1 purlwise, bring yarn to back between needles; rep from *, end k3.

Row 2 K1, bring yarn to front between needles, sl 1 purlwise, bring yarn to back between needles, *k3, bring yarn to front between needles, sl 1 purlwise, bring yarn to back between needles; rep from *, end k1.

Rep rows 1 and 2 for sl st rib.

Stitch Glossary

Sl 1 k-st with yo With yarn at front, sl next k st purlwise to RH needle, wrap yarn over RH needle and around to front again.

Sl 1 p-st with yo With yarn at front, sl next p st purlwise to RH needle, wrap yarn over RH needle to back for yarn over, ready to work next knit st.

2-st decrease K2tog (next knit st with yarn over tog with foll p st), slip st back to LH needle, pass the foll k st with yarn over on LH needle over st and off needle, slip st back to RH needle—2 sts dec'd.

Scarf

YARN (3)

- 12¼oz/350g, 875yd/798m of any DK weight wool yarn in navy (A) and light blue (B)

KNITTING NEEDLES

- One set (4) size 8 (5mm) double-pointed needles (dpn)

or size to obtain gauge

Cap

YARN (4)

- 3½oz/100g, 186yd/170m of any aran weight wool yarn in blue

KNITTING NEEDLES

- Size 7 (4.5mm) circular needle, 16"/40cm long

or size to obtain gauge

- One set (4) size 7 (4.5mm) double-pointed needles (dpn)

ADDITIONAL MATERIALS

- Stitch markers

Scarf

Side A

With A, cast on 59 sts. Work in sl st rib for 78"/198cm. Bind off in pat.

Side B

With B, cast on 59 sts. Work in sl st rib for 78"/198cm. Bind off in pat.

Finishing

With RS of each side facing and cast-on edges at lower edge, sew the 2 sides tog.

CAP

With circular needle, cast on 64 (72) sts. Join, taking care not to twist sts on needle. Place marker (pm) for beg of rnd and sl marker every rnd.

Set-up rnd *K1, sl 1 p-st with yo; rep from * around.

Rnd 1 *Sl 1 p-st with yo, k next st and yo tog; rep from * around.

Rnd 2 *P next st and yo tog, sl 1 k-st with yo; rep from * around.

Rep rnds 1 and 2 until cap measures 6½"/16.5cm from beg, end with a rnd 2.

Shape crown

Note Change to dpns when there are too few sts to fit comfortably on circular needle.

Place a marker on every 8th (9th) knit rib—4 markers placed.

Next (dec) rnd [Work in pat to knit rib before marked knit rib, work 2-st decrease] 4 times—8 sts dec'd.

Rep dec rnd every 4th rnd 2 (3) times, then every other rnd once—32 sts.

Work 1 rnd even.

Next rnd (dec) [Sl 1 p-st with yo, 2-st decrease] 8 times—16 sts.

Cut yarn leaving a long tail. Thread through rem sts, draw up and secure. ■

Paul Amato for Lvarepresents.com

Beaded Hat & Scarf

Measurements

Scarf Approx 4 x 87½"/10 x 222cm

Cap

- **Head circumference** 18"/45.5cm
- **Length** 7½"/19cm

Gauges

Scarf

- 22 sts and 26 rows to 4"/10cm over St st using size 6 (4mm) needles.

Cap

- 22 sts and 32 rnds to 4"/10cm over St st using size 6 (4mm) needles.

Take time to check your gauges.

YARN (4)

- 7oz/200g, 440yd/401m of any worsted weight wool yarn in white

KNITTING NEEDLES

- One pair size 6 (4mm) needles *or size to obtain gauge*
- One set (5) size 6 (4mm) double-pointed needles (dpns)

ADDITIONAL MATERIALS

- Approx 900 4mm silver-lined crystal beads
- Tapestry needle

Stitch Glossary

AB (add bead) Sl 1 with yarn in front, bring bead to front of sl st, k next st, leaving bead in place.

Notes

1 Beads are pre-strung on yarn and brought up to work stitch as needed.

2 Do not work beads into first or last st of row.

Scarf

String approx 400 beads on yarn. Cast on 22 sts without working beads into sts.

Row 1 (WS) *K1, p1; rep from * to end.

Row 2 *K1, p1, k1, AB; rep from * end k1, p1.

Next row and all WS rows Purl.

Row 4 *K2, AB; rep from * end k1.

Row 6 K2, *AB, k1; rep from * to end.

Cont to work in St st, adding beads in a pleasing pattern and working fewer beads into each RS row until 51 rows have been worked. Add 2 beads, placing as desired, every other row 3 times. Add 1 bead, placing as desired, every other row 21 times, then every 4th row 16 times, then every 8th row 4 times, then every 10th row 18 times.

Reverse pattern

Add bead every 8th row 4 times, and work entire sequence in reverse until 2 beads have been added every other row 3 times. Work as desired until 44 more rows have been worked. Beg with row 6, work rows in reverse through row 1. Bind off.

Hat

String 500 beads on yarn. With dpns cast on 100 sts without working beads into sts. Join, being careful not to twist sts, and pm for beg of rnd.

Rnd 1 *K1, p1; rep from *around.

Rnd 2 *K1, p1, k1, AB; rep from *around.

Rnd 3 *K2, AB; rep from * end k1.

Rnd 4 *K4, AB; rep from * around.

Rnd 5 *K3, AB; rep from * around.

Rnd 6 *K2, AB, k5, AB; rep from *end k1.

Inc rnd 7 *[K4, AB] twice, M1; rep from * around—110 sts.

Rnd 8 *K3, AB; rep from * end k2.

Inc rnd 9 *[K3, AB] twice, k2, AB, M1; rep from * around—120 sts.

Rnd 10 *K4, AB; rep from * around.

Rnd 11 *K5, AB; rep from * around.

Rnd 12 *K3, AB; rep from * around.

Rnd 13 K5, AB; rep from * around.

Rnd 14 K9, AB; rep from * around.

Rnds 15–21 Cont to add beads in every rnd, staggering placement in a pleasing fashion, approx 10 sts apart.

Rnds 22–27 Cont to add beads in every rnd, staggering placement in a pleasing fashion, approx 20 sts apart.

Rnd 28 K around without adding beads.

Rnds 29–37 Beg to add beads every other rnd only, staggering placement, approx 30 sts apart.

Shape top of cap

Set-up rnd *K24, pm; rep from * around.

Next (dec) rnd Cont to stagger placement of beads approx 20 sts apart, k to 2 sts before marker, k2tog, slip marker; rep from *around—115 sts.

Cont to stagger placement of beads approx 30 sts apart every other rnd twice, then add 1 bead every rnd, AT THE SAME TIME, rep dec rnd every rnd until 30 sts rem.

Rep dec rnd every rnd 3 times more without adding beads—15 sts. Cut yarn leaving 12"/30.5cm tail. Thread tail through open sts and draw tight. ■

Paul Amato for Lvarepresents.com

Modern Stripes Set

Measurements

Scarf Approx 9 x 66"/23 x 167.5cm

Hat

- **Head circumference (at ribbed brim)** 17"/43cm
- **Length** 10"/25.5cm

Gauges

- 18 sts and 24 rows to 4"/10cm over St st using larger needles.
- 20 sts and 26 rows to 4"/10cm over St st using smaller needles.

Take time to check your gauges.

Stitch Glossary

K2, P2 Rib

(over a multiple of 4 sts)

Row 1 *K2, p2; rep from * to end.

Row 2 K the knit sts and p the purl sts.

Rep row 2 for k2, p2 rib.

Note

Cut colors not in use for more than 4 rows.

Scarf

With larger needles and A, cast on 40 sts and work 6 rows in k2, p2 rib. Change to St st (k on RS, p on WS) and work 8 rows.

Beg Stripes

Cont in St st as foll:

[2 rows B, 2 rows A] 3 times, 2 rows A, 30 rows B, [2 rows C, 2 rows D] 3 times, 2 rows C, 20 rows A, 2 rows D, 4 rows B, 40 rows C, 4 rows B, [2 rows D, 2 rows A] 3 times, [2 rows C, 2 rows A] 3 times, [2 rows B, 2 rows A] 3 times, 44 rows A, [2 rows A, 2 rows B] 3 times, [2 rows A, 2 rows C] 3 times, [2 rows A, 2 rows D] 3 times, 4 rows B, 40 rows C, 4 rows B, 2 rows D, 20 rows A, [2 rows C, 2 rows D] 3 times, 2 rows C, 30 rows B, 4 rows A, [2 rows B, 2 rows A] 3 times, 6 rows A. Cont with A, work 6 rows in k2, p2 rib. Bind off.

YARN (4)

- 3½oz/100g, 220yd/201m of any worsted weight wool in dark gray (A), coral (B), light gray (C), and light peach (D)

KNITTING NEEDLES

- One pair each size 7 and 8 (4.5 and 5mm) needles *or size to obtain gauge*

ADDITIONAL MATERIALS

- Tapestry needle

Hat

With smaller needles and A, cast on 90 sts and work 6 rows in k2, p2 rib. Change to St st and work 4 rows.

Beg Stripes

Cont in St st and work in stripes as foll: [2 rows C, 2 rows A] 3 times, 2 rows A, join B to complete hat, AT THE SAME TIME, when piece measures 7¼"/18.5cm from beg, end with WS row, shape crown.

Shape Crown

Row 1 (RS) *K7, k2tog; rep from* to end—80 sts.

Row 2 (and all WS rows) Purl.

Row 3 *K6, K2tog; rep from * to end—70 sts.

Row 5 *K5, k2tog; rep from * to end—60 sts.

Row 7 *K4, k2tog; rep from * to end—50 sts.

Row 9 *K3, k2tog; rep from * to end—40 sts.

Row 11 *K2, k2tog; rep from * to end—30 sts.

Row 13 *K1, k2tog; rep from * to end—20 sts.

Row 15 *K2tog; rep from * to end—10 sts.

Row 16 P10. Cut yarn, leaving 12"/30.5cm tail. Thread tapestry needle with tail and draw through rem sts. Sew seam. ■

David Lazarus

Olive Stripes

Measurements

Scarf Approx 9 x 66"/23 x 167.5cm

Cap

- **Head circumference (at ribbed brim)** 17"/43cm
- **Length** 7¼"/18.5cm

Gauge

- 18 sts and 24 rows to 4"/10cm over St st using larger needles.
- 20 sts and 26 rows to 4"/10cm over St st using smaller needles.

Take time to check your gauges.

K2, P2 Rib

(over a multiple of 4 sts)

Row 1*K2, p2; rep from * to end.

Row 2 K the knit sts and p the purl sts.

Rep row 2 for k2, p2 rib.

Note

Cut colors not in use for more than 4 rows.

Scarf

With larger needles and A, cast on 40 sts and work 6 rows in k2, p2 rib. Change to St st (k on RS, p on WS) and work 8 rows.

Beg Stripes

Cont in St st as foll: [4 rows B, 4 rows A] twice, 4 rows B, [2 rows C, 2 rows B] twice, 50 rows C, 12 rows D, 6 rows A, 12 rows D, 2 rows B, [2 rows D, 2 rows B] 3 times, [2 rows C, 2 rows B] 3 times, [2 rows A, 2 rows B] 3 times, 20 rows more with B, 40 rows D, 22 rows B, [2 rows A, 2 rows B] 3 times, [2 rows C, 2 rows B] 3 times, [2 rows D, 2 rows B] 3 times, 12 rows D, 6 rows A, 12 rows D, 50 rows C, [2 rows B, 2 rows C] twice, [4 rows B, 4 rows A] twice, 4 rows B, 8 rows A. Cont with A, change to k2, p2 rib and work 6 rows. Bind off.

YARN (4)

- 3½oz/100g, 220yd/201m of any worsted weight wool in yellow heather (A), gray heather (B), olive heather (C), green heather (D)

KNITTING NEEDLES

- One pair each size 7 and 8 (4.5 and 5mm) needles *or size to obtain gauge*

ADDITIONAL MATERIALS

- Tapestry needle

Cap

With smaller needles and A, cast on 90 sts and work 6 rows in k2, p2 rib.

Beg Stripes

Change to St st and work stripes as foll: [2 rows B, 2 rows A] 3 times, [2 rows B, 2 rows D] 3 times, [2 rows B, 2 rows C] 3 times, cont in B until cap is complete, at the same time, when cap measures 4½"/11.5cm from beg, shape crown.

Shape Crown

Row 1 (RS) *K7, k2tog; rep from * to end—80 sts.

Row 2 (and all WS rows) Purl.

Row 3 *K6, K2tog; rep from * to end—70 sts.

Row 5 *K5, k2tog; rep from * to end—60 sts.

Row 7 *K4, k2tog; rep from * to end—50 sts.

Row 9 *K3, k2tog; rep from * to end—40 sts.

Row 11 *K2, k2tog; rep from * to end—30 sts.

Row 13 *K1, k2tog; rep from * to end—20 sts.

Row 15 *K2tog; rep from * to end—10 sts.

Row 16 P10. Cut yarn, leaving 12"/30.5cm tail. Thread tapestry needle with tail and draw through rem sts. Sew seam. ■

David Lazarus

David Lazarus

Purple Stripes

Measurements
Scarf Approx 9 x 66"/23 x 167.5cm
Cap
- **Head circumference (at ribbed brim)** 17"/43cm
- **Length** 7¼"/18.5cm

Gauges
- 18 sts and 24 rows to 4"/10cm over St st using larger needles.
- 20 sts and 26 rows to 4"/10cm over St st using smaller needles.

Take time to check your gauges.

Stitch Glossary
K2, P2 Rib
(over a multiple of 4 sts)
Row 1 *K2, p2; rep from * to end.
Row 2 K the knit sts and p the purl sts.
Rep row 2 for k2, p2 rib.

Note
Cut colors not in use for more than 4 rows.

YARN (4)
- 3½oz/100g, 220yd/201m of any worsted weight wool in purple (A), gray heather (B), lt purple heather (C), gray/purple heather (D)

KNITTING NEEDLES
- One pair each size 7 and 8 (4.5 and 5mm) needles *or size to obtain gauge*

ADDITIONAL MATERIALS
- Tapestry needle

Scarf
With larger needles and A, cast on 40 sts and work 6 rows in k2, p2 rib. Change to St st (k on RS, p on WS) and work 8 rows.

Beg Stripes
Cont in St st as foll: [4 rows B, 4 rows A] twice, 4 rows B, [2 rows C, 2 rows B] twice, 50 rows C, 12 rows D, 6 rows A, 12 rows D, 2 rows B, [2 rows D, 2 rows B] 3 times, [2 rows C, 2 rows B] 3 times, [2 rows A, 2 rows B] 3 times, 20 rows more with B, 40 rows D, 22 rows B, [2 rows A, 2 rows B] 3 times, [2 rows C, 2 rows B] 3 times, [2 rows D, 2 rows B] 3 times, 12 rows D, 6 rows A, 12 rows D, 50 rows C, [2 rows B, 2 rows C] twice, [4 rows B, 4 rows A] twice, 4 rows B, 8 rows A. Cont with A, change to k2, p2 rib and work 6 rows. Bind off.

Cap
With smaller needles and A, cast on 90 sts and work 6 rows in k2, p2 rib.

Beg Stripes
Change to St st and work stripes as foll: [2 rows B, 2 rows A] 3 times, [2 rows B, 2 rows D] 3 times, [2 rows B, 2 rows C] 3 times, cont in B until cap is complete, at the same time, when cap measures 4½"/11.5cm from beg, shape crown.

Shape Crown
Row 1 (RS) *K7, k2tog; rep from * to end—80 sts.
Row 2 (and all WS rows) Purl.
Row 3 *K6, K2tog; rep from * to end—70 sts.
Row 5 *K5, k2tog; rep from * to end—60 sts.
Row 7 *K4, k2tog; rep from * to end—50 sts.
Row 9 *K3, k2tog; rep from * to end—40 sts.
Row 11 *K2, k2tog; rep from * to end—30 sts.
Row 13 *K1, k2tog; rep from * to end—20 sts.
Row 15 *K2tog; rep from * to end—10 sts.
Row 16 P10. Cut yarn, leaving 12"/30.5cm tail. Thread tapestry needle with tail and draw through rem sts. Sew seam. ■

David Lazarus

Berry Stripes

Measurements

Scarf Approx 9 x 66"/23 x 167.5cm

Hat

- **Head circumference (at ribbed brim)** 17"/43cm
- **Length** 11½"/29cm

Gauges

- 18 sts and 24 rows to 4"/10cm over St st using larger needles.
- 21 sts and 31 rows to 4"/10cm over Sl st pat using larger needles.

Take time to check your gauges.

K2, P2 Rib

(over a multiple of 4 sts)

Row 1 *K2, p2; rep from * to end.

Row 2 K the knit sts and p the purl sts.

Rep row 2 for k2, p2 rib.

Slip Stitch Pattern

(over an odd number of sts)

Row 1 (RS) With B, k1, *sl 1 wyif, k1; rep from * to end.

Row 2 With B, purl.

Row 3 With C, k1, *sl 1 wyib, k1; rep from * to end.

Row 4 With C, purl.

Row 5 With D, k1, *sl 1 wyif, k1; rep from * to end.

Row 6 With D, purl.

Rows 7 and 8 With B, rep rows 3 and 4.

Rows 9 and 10 With C, rep rows 1 and 2.

Rows 11 and 12 With D, rep rows 3 and 4.

Rep rows 1–12 for slip st pat.

Note

Cut colors not in use for more than 4 rows.

YARN

- 3½oz/100g, 220yd/201m of any worsted weight wool in rose (A), fuchsia (B), pale pink (C), and brown (D)

KNITTING NEEDLES

- One pair each size 7 and 8 (4.5 and 5mm) needles *or size to obtain gauge*

ADDITIONAL MATERIALS

- Tapestry needle

David Lazarus

Scarf

With larger needles and A, cast on 40 sts and work 6 rows in k2, p2 rib.

Next row (RS) Inc 1 st, k39—41 sts. Purl 1 row.

Beg Pat

*Work rows 1–12 of sl st pat 3 times. Change to A and St st and work 12 rows. Rep from * 8 times more. Work rows 1–12 of sl st pat 3 times. K 1 row A.

Next (dec) row (WS) P39, p2tog—40 sts. Cont with A, change to k2, p2 rib and work 6 rows. Bind off.

Cap

With smaller needles and A, cast on 90 sts and work 6 rows in k2, p2 rib. Change to larger needles.

Next row (RS) Inc 1 st, k89—91 sts. Purl 1 row. Cont with St st and A, work 2 rows.

Beg Pat

Work rows 1–12 of sl st pat 6 times.

Shape Crown

With A, shape crown as foll:

Row 1 (RS) *K5, k2tog; rep from * to end—78 sts.

Row 2 and all WS rows Purl.

Row 3 *K4, k2tog; rep from * to end—65 sts.

Row 5 *K3, k2tog; rep from * to end—52 sts.

Row 7 *K2, k2tog—39 sts.

Row 9 *K1, k2tog; rep from * to end—26 sts.

Row 11 [K2tog] 13 times—13 sts.

Row 12 P13. Cut yarn, leaving 12"/30.5cm tail. Thread tapestry needle with tail and draw through rem sts. Sew seam. ■

Gold Stripes

Measurements

Scarf Approx 9 x 66"/23 x 167.5cm

Hat

- **Head circumference (at ribbed brim)** 17"/43cm
- **Length** 11½"/29cm

Gauges

- 18 sts and 24 rows to 4"/10cm over St st using larger needles.
- 21 sts and 31 rows to 4"/10cm over Sl st pat using larger needles.

Take time to check your gauges.

K2, P2 Rib

(over a multiple of 4 sts)

Row 1 *K2, p2; rep from * to end.

Row 2 K the knit sts and p the purl sts.

Rep row 2 for k2, p2 rib.

Slip Stitch Pattern

(over an odd number of sts)

Row 1 (RS) With B, k1, *sl 1 wyif, k1; rep from * to end.

Row 2 With B, purl.

Row 3 With C, k1, *sl 1 wyib, k1; rep from * to end.

Row 4 With C, purl.

Row 5 With D, k1, *sl 1 wyif, k1; rep from * to end.

Row 6 With D, purl.

Rows 7 and 8 With B, rep rows 3 and 4.

Rows 9 and 10 With C, rep rows 1 and 2.

Rows 11 and 12 With D, rep rows 3 and 4.

Rep rows 1–12 for slip st pat.

Note

Cut colors not in use for more than 4 rows.

YARN (4)

- 3½oz/100g, 220yd/201m of any worsted weight wool in yellow (A), orange (B), pale yellow (C), olive green (D

KNITTING NEEDLE

- One pair each size 7 and 8 (4.5 and 5mm) needles *or size to obtain gauge*

ADDITIONAL MATERIALS

- Tapestry needle

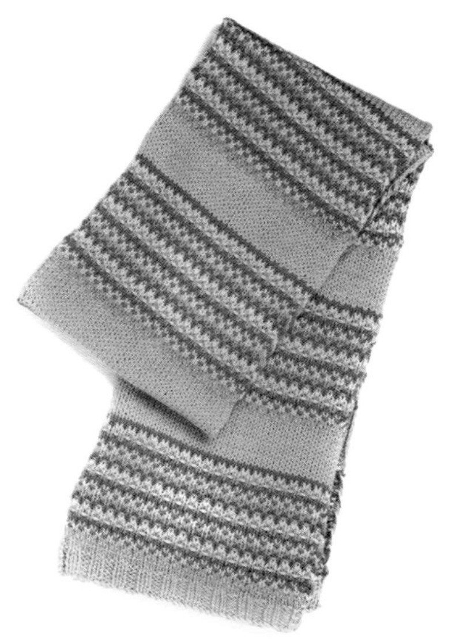

David Lazarus

*Work rows 1–12 of sl st pat 3 times. Change to A and St st and work 12 rows. Rep from * 8 times more. Work rows 1–12 of sl st pat 3 times. K 1 row A.

Next (dec) row (WS) P39, p2tog—40 sts.

Cont with A, change to k2, p2 rib and work 6 rows. Bind off.

Cap

With smaller needles and A, cast on 90 sts and work 6 rows in k2, p2 rib. Change to larger needles.

Next row (RS) Inc 1 st, k89—91 sts.

Purl 1 row. Cont with St st and A, work 2 rows.

Beg Pat

Work rows 1–12 of sl st pat 6 times.

Shape Crown

With A shape crown as foll:

Row 1 (RS) *K5, k2tog; rep from * to end—78 sts.

Row 2 and all WS rows Purl.

Row 3 *K4, k2tog; rep from * to end—65 sts.

Row 5 *K3, k2tog; rep from * to end—52 sts.

Row 7 *K2, k2tog—39 sts.

Row 9 *K1, k2tog; rep from * to end—26 sts.

Row 11 [K2tog] 13 times—13 sts.

Row 12 P13. Cut yarn, leaving 12"/30.5cm tail. Thread tapestry needle with tail and draw through rem sts. Sew seam. ■

Teal Stripes

Measurements

Scarf

- **Approximately** 9 x 66"/23 x 167.5cm

Hat

- **Head circumference (at ribbed brim)** 17"/43cm
- **Length** 10"/25.5cm

Gauges

- 18 sts and 24 rows to 4"/10cm over St st using larger needles.
- 20 sts and 26 rows to 4"/10cm over St st using smaller needles.

Take time to check your gauges.

K2, P2 Rib

(over a multiple of 4 sts)

Row 1 *K2, p2; rep from * to end.

Row 2 K the knit sts and p the purl sts.

Rep row 2 for k2, p2 rib.

Note

Cut colors not in use for more than 4 rows.

YARN (4)

- 3½oz/100g, 220yd/201m of any worsted weight wool in dark gray heather (A), blue heather (B), light blue heather (C), aqua (D)

KNITTING NEEDLES

- One pair each size 7 and 8 (4.5 and 5mm) needles *or size to obtain gauge*

ADDITIONAL MATERIALS

- Tapestry needle

Scarf

With larger needles and A, cast on 40 sts and work 6 rows in k2, p2 rib. Change to St st (k on RS, p on WS) and work 8 rows.

Beg Stripes

Cont in St st as foll:

[2 rows B, 2 rows A] 3 times, 2 rows A, 30 rows B, [2 rows C, 2 rows D] 3 times, 2 rows C, 20 rows A, 2 rows D, 4 rows B, 40 rows C, 4 rows B, [2 rows D, 2 rows A] 3 times, [2 rows C, 2 rows A] 3 times, [2 rows B, 2 rows A] 3 times, 44 rows A, [2 rows A, 2 rows B] 3 times, [2 rows A, 2 rows C] 3 times, [2 rows A, 2 rows D] 3 times, 4 rows B, 40 rows C, 4 rows B, 2 rows D, 20 rows A, [2 rows C, 2 rows D] 3 times, 2 rows C, 30 rows B, 4 rows A, [2 rows B, 2 rows A] 3 times, 6 rows A. Cont with A, work 6 rows in k2, p2 rib. Bind off.

Hat

With smaller needles and A, cast on 90 sts and work 6 rows in k2, p2 rib. Change to St st and work 4 rows.

Beg Stripes

Cont in St st and work in stripes as foll:

[2 rows C, 2 rows A] 3 times, 2 rows A, join B to complete hat, AT THE SAME TIME, when piece measures 7¼"/18.5cm from beg, end with WS row, shape crown.

Shape Crown

Row 1 (RS) *K7, k2tog; rep from * to end—80 sts.

Row 2 (and all WS rows) Purl.

Row 3 *K6, K2tog; rep from * to end—70 sts.

Row 5 *K5, k2tog; rep from * to end—60 sts.

Row 7 *K4, k2tog; rep from * to end—50 sts.

Row 9 *K3, k2tog; rep from * to end—40 sts.

Row 11 *K2, k2tog; rep from * to end—30 sts.

Row 13 *K1, k2tog; rep from * to end—20 sts.

Row 15 *K2tog; rep from * to end—10 sts.

Row 16 P10. Cut yarn, leaving 12"/30.5cm tail. Thread tapestry needle with tail and draw through rem sts. Sew seam. ■

David Lazarus

Seed Stitch & Cables Set

Measurements

Scarf

- 7" x 62"/18cm x 157.5cm

Hat

- **Circumference** 17"/43cm

Gauges

Scarf

- 14 sts and 24 rows to 4"/10cm over seed st.

Hat

- 18 sts and 24 rows to 4"/10cm over seed st in the round using larger dpns.

Take time to check your gauges.

Stitch Glossary

4-st LC Sl 2 sts to cn and hold to front, k2, k2 from cn.

LC & Dec Sl 2 sts to cn and hold to front, k2tog, k2 from cn.

SK2P Sl 1, k2tog, psso.

S2KP Sl 2 knitwise, k1, pass 2 slip sts over.

Scarf

Cast on 25 sts. Work in seed st as foll:

Row 1 (RS) K1, *k1, p1; rep from * to end.

Rows 2–7 Sl 1 knitwise, *k1, p1; rep from * to end.

Next (inc) row (WS) Sl 1 knitwise, [k1, p1] twice, pm, [k1, p1] twice, pm, [k1, p1] twice, M1, k1, p1, k1, pm, [p1, k1] twice, pm, [p1, k1] twice, p1—26 sts.

Beg cable pat

Note Cont to work from text or from scarf chart, rep rows 5–8 until approx 60"/152.5cm from beg, end with row 8.

Rows 1 and 3 (RS) Sl 1 knitwise, [k1, p1] twice, slip marker (sl m), k2, yo, ssk, sl m, p2, k4, p2, k2, sl m, yo, ssk, sl m, [p1, k1] twice, p1.

Scarf

YARN

- 12¼oz/350g, 385yd/350m of any bulky weight wool in navy

KNITTING NEEDLES

- Size 8 (5mm) needles *or size to obtain gauge*

Hat

YARN

- 5¼oz/150g, 165yd/150m in navy

KNITTING NEEDLES

- One set (5) each size 7 and 8 (4.5 and 5mm) double-pointed needles (dpns) *or size to obtain gauge*

ADDITIONAL MATERIALS

- Cable needle (cn)
- Tapestry needle

Row 2 and all WS rows Sl 1 knitwise, [k1, p1] twice, sl m, p2, yo, p2tog, sl m, k2, p4, k2, sl m, p2, yo, p2tog, sl m, end [p1, k1] twice, p1.

Row 5 Sl 1 knitwise, [k1, p1] twice, sl m, k2, yo, ssk, sl m, p2, 4-st LC, p2, sl m, k2, yo, ssk, sl m, end [p1, k1] twice, p1.

Row 7 Sl 1 knitwise, [k1, p1] twice, sl m, k2, yo, ssk, sl m, p2, k4, p2, sl m, k2, yo, ssk, sl m, end [p1, k1] twice, p1.

Row 8 Rep row 2. Remove markers.

Next (dec) row (RS) Sl 1 knitwise, [k1, p1] six times, k2tog, [p1, k1] 5 times, p1—25 sts.

Work rows 2–7 of seed st. Bind off in pat.

Hat

With smaller dpns, cast on 75 sts. Place marker and join for knitting in the round, taking care not to twist sts. Work as foll:

Rnds 1, 3 and 4 *P2, [k1, p1] 3 times, k1, p2, k4; rep from * to marker.

Rnd 2 *P2, [k1, p1] 3 times, k1, p2, 4-st LC; rep from * to marker.

Work rnds 1–4 once more. Change to larger dpns.

Beg cable pat

Note Rep rnds 1–4 from text or from hat chart until 9 cable twists have been worked from beg.

Rnds 1, 3 and 4 *P2, k2, p1, k1, p1, k2, p2, k4; rep from * to marker.

Rnd 2 *P2, [k1, p1] 3 times, k1, p2, 4-st LC; rep from * to marker.

Crown shaping

Rnd 1 *P2, ssk, p1, k1, p1, k2tog, p2, k2; rep from * to marker—65 sts.

Rnd 2 *P2, k2, p1, k2, p2, 4-st LC; rep from * to marker.

Rnd 3 *P2, ssk, k1, k2tog, p2, k4; rep from * to marker—55 sts.

Rnd 4 *P2, k1, p1, k1 p2, k4; rep from * to marker.

Rnd 5 *P2, sl 1 purlwise, k2tog, psso, p2, k4; rep from * to marker—45 sts.

Rnd 6 *P2, k1, p2, 4-st LC; rep from * to marker.

Rnd 7 *P1, sl 2 knitwise, k1, p2sso, p1, k4; rep from * to marker—35 sts.

Rnd 8 *P1, k1, p1, k4; rep from * to marker.

Rnd 9 *Sl 2 knitwise, k1, p2sso, k4; rep from * to marker—25 sts.

Rnd 10 *K1, LC & Dec; rep from * to marker—20 sts.

Rnd 11 *Sl 2 knitwise, k1, p2sso, k1; rep from * to marker—10 sts.

Cut yarn, leaving a 12"/30.5cm tail, thread through rem sts, cinch tightly to close. ■

Jenny Acheson

Seed Stitch & Cables Set

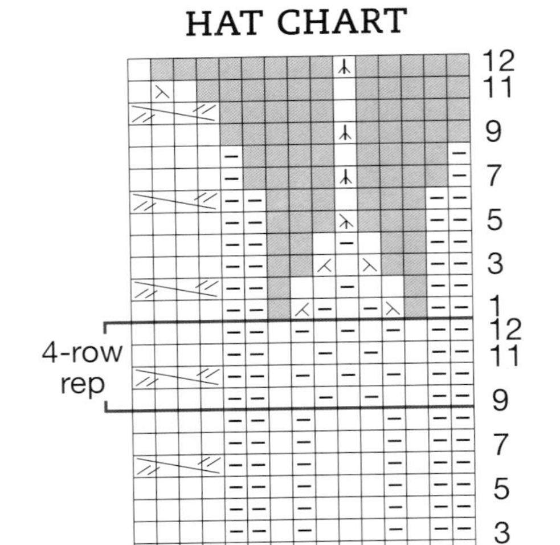

STITCH KEY

- K on RS, p on WS
- P on RS, k on WS
- Sl 1 knitwise
- Yarn over
- Ssk
- K2tog
- P2tog
- Sk2p
- S2kp
- No stitch
- 4-st LC

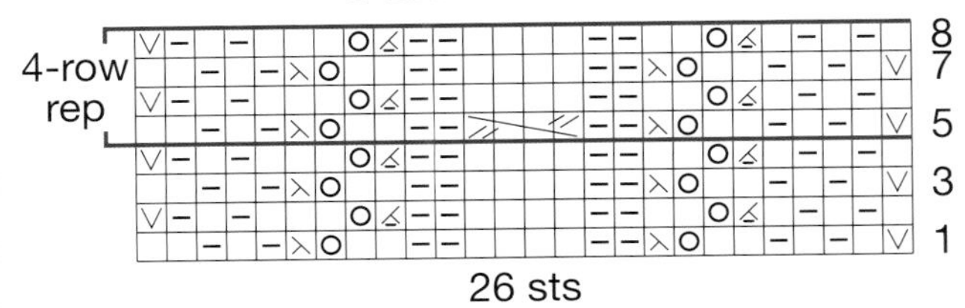